THE HOPE IN LEAVING

THE HOPE IN LEAVING

a memoir

Barbara Williams

SEVEN STORIES PRESS
New York • Oakland

A Seven Stories Press First Edition

Seven Stories Press
140 Watts Street
New York, NY 10013
www.sevenstories.com

College professors may order examination copies of Seven Stories Press titles
for free. To order, visit http://www.sevenstories.com/textbook or send a fax on
school letterhead to (212) 226-1411.

Book design by Elizabeth DeLong

Library of Congress Cataloging-in-Publication Data
Names: Williams, Barbara, 1953-
Title: The hope in leaving : a memoir / Barbara Williams.
Description: First edition. | New York : Seven Stories Press, 2016.
Identifiers: LCCN 2015029675 | ISBN 9781609806729 (hardcover)
Subjects: LCSH: Williams, Barbara, 1953---Childhood and youth. | Williams,
    Barbara, 1953---Family. | Coming of age--British Columbia. |
    Loggers--Family relationships--British Columbia. | Logging--Social
    aspects--British Columbia. | Migrant laborers' families--British
    Columbia--Biography. | Poor families--British Columbia--Biography. |
    Dysfunctional families--British Columbia--Biography. | British
    Columbia--Biography. | Actresses--Canada--Biography. | BISAC: BIOGRAPHY &
    AUTOBIOGRAPHY / Personal Memoirs. | BIOGRAPHY & AUTOBIOGRAPHY /
    Entertainment & Performing Arts. | BIOGRAPHY & AUTOBIOGRAPHY / Women.
Classification: LCC CT310.W49 A3 2016 | DDC 306.85086/94209711--dc23
LC record available at http://lccn.loc.gov/2015029675

Printed in the United States

9 8 7 6 5 4 3 2 1

DEDICATION

To Jean

ACKNOWLEDGMENTS

A huge thank-you to Dan Simon, my wonderful
editor Jesse Ruddock, Ruth Weiner, Liz DeLong
and the team at Seven Stories Press.

For their feedback and guidance I thank Bill Clegg,
Ottessa Moshfegh, Jack Grapes, my writing group
and members of the Actor's Gym.

Love to Tom, Liam and my mom,
for understanding.

Leaving

Randy is sitting across from me with a hunting knife lying on his lap. We're in a field with high grass, where we used to play commandos. It's getting dark and I want to leave, but I'm afraid to turn my back on him. "Can I have it?" I ask.

His hands lift away, inviting me to grab the knife. We both know I'm not fast enough. He's always been faster.

Keeping eye contact with him, I slowly stand. He rises too, gripping the knife with the blade down, and we face each other in a static duel.

"Let's not do this," I urge him. "Let's go."

His face questions me. He wants to trust me.

"It's time to go home."

His eyes get watery. He doesn't really want to play this game.

"Let me have the knife," I say.

He's ashamed. "I'm sorry," he says, lifting his arm and opening his palm.

In one move I grab the knife and push the blade deep into

his stomach. I see in his eyes that he knew this is how it would end.

And then I see the ceiling above my head and the room that is emptied of everything except my backpack and my sleeping bag that I'm zipped into. And I remember that I'm leaving today.

I've had a variation of this dream with Randy and the hunting knife a few times now. Each time, I wake up with the overwhelming sense that I have to leave. This is the first time I've killed my brother.

There's an explosion of rain on the roof and I'm compelled to check my car. It's packed with all my belongings. I'm driving it to my mother's house this morning, then catching a red-eye to Toronto where I have a job waiting for me. I'm giving everything to Randy. A bribe to let me go. I start to cry. I guess I'm anxious about leaving, worried about Randy. When I go outside, my car is gone.

By 5am, I'm standing at an impound station on Skid Row, where my car was towed after it was found parked on a sidewalk. Probably some teenage joyride, and I've done worse, but it's unfair that I have to pay the ninety bucks to redeem it.

The rain is still coming down. An old man too long in his cups has thrown up on the sidewalk and I can't be sure he didn't splatter my sleeping bag, so I give it to him. He wanders away singing. I don't mind drunks, they're harmless, as long as they aren't raising you.

We used to come here when I was little. It's Dad's turf, where he gets his logging work—Skid Row hotel bars are his hiring halls, since you have to be drunk to sign up for the kind of work he does. We would sit in the car outside darkened doorways while Dad ran in "for just a minute." Then we'd wait for hours with scary faces leering in at us, skinny men with mashed-up noses and cuts over their eyes, and women with pasty skin and dark-red lipstick smeared around rotting teeth. At closing time they would slither by our car, cursing, crying, and hitting each other. Finally Dad would stagger out and we'd hold on tight for the blackout drive to wherever we happened to be living at the time.

My guitar and suitcase are missing, the only things I was planning to take to Toronto. Everything else is here, just a little defiled. Everything but my windshield wipers that have been ripped off, the little shits. It's still pouring and I can barely see as I start driving. I keep my windows down to reduce the fog and I race to the ferry at an insanely reckless clip, bawling as much as the rain. I can see more the faster I go, speed making the water thin against the glass.

On the ferry I sequester myself by a starboard window for the comfort of a familiar view. My stomach is a twisted mess. Hot tea and food might help but it's too much effort. I fix my eyes on the gray seascape and surrender to the storm. Disappointed tourists stare through the windows, hoping some errant orca might sail out of the gloom. Usually I love this trip. No matter the weather, I go out on the upper deck and breathe the best air in the world. Not that I've breathed the air in other places, but I know this air is the best.

With my stomach still churning, I go outside and the rain soaks my clothes. The dream with Randy replays in my head.

"I'm sorry," he says. "I'm sorry." Then the sun appears. The ferry whistle blows loud and long to announce our approach to Active Pass, and there's silence in our wake.

Jack and Simone

There was an overturned baby carriage impaled on a dock piling when my mother first arrived in Zeballos Harbor on the Northwest coast of Vancouver Island in 1953. She was nineteen and pregnant with me, her second child.

The constant roll of the open ocean, diesel fumes, and the hot hum of the tugboat's engine kept her in a nauseous stupor. She was having a bad pregnancy and those sea legs that she kept being assured would come had not arrived. Her legs ached. A cluster of veins at her ankle had popped out overnight.

Randy was passed out in the bent arm of the skipper's wife, who sat turning the pages of an old magazine, inured to the sickening atmosphere of the cabin. Mom's pregnancy with Randy had been easy, and his existence had sprung new instincts in her. Mothering was a joy. But she was not having a good time with me. She pulled herself up and tottered out to the deck, where the rain on her face brought some relief.

Dad was standing watch at the stern, gracefully swaying

with the pitch of the boat. His hands floated outward for balance and Mom thought of Gene Kelly in *Singing in the Rain*, the last movie she'd seen, and then she thought of her sister, who got all the dance and music lessons.

Beyond the tugboat's wake, their new home, a prefab float house not much bigger than her dad's toolshed, resisted being towed. The skipper, John Riggs, shouted out from behind the wheel, "You know, Simone, Indians here believe that all the weather is the mood of their ancestors." That made her stomach unsettle again. "I think they're letting us through today."

"Thank you Grandfather," Dad said with an exaggerated Native accent, looking up to the heavens, "and your grandfather and all your grandmothers and all the sons of your sisters that you fathered." Mom forced a little ha-ha. She didn't think it was funny when Jack did his mock Indian chief, particularly because his grandmother was Lakota Sioux.

"They can still change their minds," John cautioned. "Last year a westerly kicked up when I was fifty feet from the dock. I was towing three houses and one broke loose and got smashed to bits on the rocks."

"Now don't get Simone in a panic," Dad said. "She's only ever been caught in a ripple over Lake Louise."

Mom wanted to say something clever but nothing came to her.

A pillow of mist blew away and suddenly they were entering Zeballos Harbor. Dad threw a dinghy off the boat and rowed over to the boom carrying the house. A dozen plain structures exactly like the one they were towing formed the float-camp they were about to join.

Mom was near-sighted and thought she might be seeing a totem pole for the first time. The skipper's wife stepped on deck, still holding the sleeping Randy, "Ah Jesus, they haven't taken that damn buggy down yet."

Mom squinted and the baby carriage came into focus, overturned on a piling by the dock, the hood in tatters and wheel spokes rusted.

"It's tragic," the skipper's wife went on. "The mother puts a little baby girl in the buggy with a bottle of orange juice. For one thing, you don't give a baby orange juice, their teeth will come in rotten, and you never leave it alone with a bottle. You know that, don't you?" Mom nodded, pretending to know.

"But that's what she did and the poor darling chokes to death. Can you imagine? I couldn't go to the funeral, just ripped me up, but the dad, name's Geordie, you'll meet him—both of them, perfectly nice people—he went kinda nuts and goes running through town with the empty buggy, all the way down the dock and throws it off. And that's where it landed, and nobody has taken the godforsaken thing down."

Mom was ready to throw up and carefully got down on all fours, holding her head off the stern.

Mom sat up in the watery night. By a bare lightbulb, she wrote a letter to her father, the continuation of a two-year deception. Her father was a British Army officer, a wounded veteran of the First World War, a stiff-upper-lip proper gentlemen. He'd been thrown off-kilter three years before when his wife committed suicide and was unsure of how to deal with a teenage daughter. His older daughters had left home.

Thinking it would be a more comforting environment, he sent Mom to live with family friends. When the father's kind gestures to comfort her turned lewd, Mom didn't know how to defend herself. She ran away and headed to Vancouver. She found a place to stay with Sara, an acquaintance of Mom's older sister, Tinker. Her father knew nothing about why she fled and was not pleased with her dropout status. Mom eventually appeased him by enrolling in the Vancouver Vocational Institute. Then she met Dad at a party and traded a future vocation for immediate affection.

The ancestors grew agitated. A loose cup shattered on the floor. Mom strained to pick up the pieces. She nudged a snoring Jack to the edge of the bed and lay down on her back. Outside, the logs moaned as they chafed against each other, sounding like humans. It was vulgar, like unstifled lovemaking in a thin-walled motel. A storm was rising, the chafing quickened.

"Simone," Dad said, awake and sitting up, "the bed's wet."

The men made a chair of their arms and awkwardly carried Mom across the slippery logs, with John's wife holding her husband's jacket for support and gripping Randy in her other arm. Fleet rain assaulted their faces.

"You all right, Barb?" John said, and Mom realized his wife's name was Barb.

"I'm all right, everyone's all right. The hospital's just an hour away, Simone, don't you worry." Mom groaned to think she'd have to endure this pain another minute.

They set her on the grungy bed in the boat's cabin.

Randy put his face next to Mom's. Barb stroked his head but he never took his eyes from his mother.

"I'm just going to go on deck, help John . . . navigate . . . not much I can do here . . . unless you, ah, think . . . ?" Dad stammered.

Barb gave him a look like she wanted to hit him.

"Go . . . I'm . . . *ahhh* . . . I'm *fiiii* . . ." Mom's last word was swallowed by a contraction.

"Never been better, huh?" Dad couldn't help but quip, and Mom expelled a laugh in spite of herself.

Randy sat up hoping Mom was going to play now, but she grunted out an ugly sound that made his lower lip quiver. A wave smacked the boat and he tumbled to the floor.

Barb reached out and cradled him but he bawled for his mother, a goose egg rising on his forehead. Mom stretched out her arms and he flew into them, thudding on her churning belly.

Barb braced her thick body around them both to minimize the turbulence. Mom took a deep breath and silently rode out the next contraction.

"You're so blessed," Barb squeezed her hand and Mom remembered her mentioning that she had no children, which seemed to make her sad. For a moment Mom considered offering this baby to Barb but that was crazy. She had to push away crazy thoughts. Barb had those big hands like her mother's, capable hands that made you feel safe, that pulled people she hardly knew into her chest for loving hugs, hands that fluttered and tapped as she tried to find words in English. "*Comment tu dis . . .* ?" her mother said so often.

Whatever pain Mom felt for the rest of her labor was

barely expressed, except for the periodic wince that would trigger Barb to grip her hand tighter and Randy to grip her neck.

The tugboat tooted its horn. "Thank God we're here," Barb announced. "We're in Esperanza. You know what Esperanza means?"

Mom relaxed and I slid out.

"Hope," Barb told her.

I imagine Dad walking across the little bridge over the stream that divided Esperanza. The hotel wasn't open yet but he had to get away from the hospital. Missionaries gave him the creeps. They called themselves The Shantymen— sounded like a swing quartet, he thought. Doc Maclean and The Shantymen.

The Reverend Doctor had gone at him, urging him to get both kids baptized.

"A person gets baptized every day out here," Jack countered.

"If not for you, then for the children," the doctor insisted.

"When they're old enough they can choose."

It annoyed the crap out of Dad that Doctor Maclean held me up like he had delivered me when Barb was the hero.

"She's a good old girl," he mused, "too wide in the beams to be a looker, but decent enough."

It made Barb's day when Dad named me after her. He thought it was a fine name.

Three Native men were lying on the hotel porch, grounded by the storm. Dad sat on the stairs. One man sensed Dad's presence and sat up without opening his eyes. He was wearing a bowler hat and a tweed suit with dirt-frayed cuffs reeking of last night's alcohol and years of spilt eulachon oil. Nootka, Dad figured. He could discern the subtleties between different tribes by how their features were set. Dad could pass for a dark white man, but Native people always pegged him as Indian.

Even if the six rooms in the hotel weren't taken, they wouldn't be open to these men. "No prizes for being Indian," Dad was known to say. Loggers were Dad's tribe. Loose cannons, ex-cons, men on the lam, addicts kicking a habit, loners, and misfit jokers with a tendency toward excess who had the wherewithal to roust up a pair of caulk boots, surrender to the isolation, put in ten hours of work a day, and keep their noses clean and out of other people's business. Those were his people.

Mrs. Elaine Moore opened the front door holding a broom like she was about to sweep away the human refuse.

"Come on guys, time to get on your way," she said, mustering a tolerant tone.

"They're going to have breakfast with me," Dad said, standing up.

"Oh good morning, Jack." She'd been charmed by Jack before. "Awfully early to be down the Inlet?"

"Simone just had a baby." He motioned with his thumb to the hospital.

"Well, God bless her," said Mrs. Moore with a trace of pity.

The three men lined up at the door.

"I can't let them in, Jack. I can't run a business when people don't pay for services."

"Put whatever they owe on my tab, you know I'm good for it."

Mom was half sitting with me tightly swaddled and propped against her bent knees. I was small, just four pounds. After coming through a squamish in Hecate Channel and being born in Esperanza, Dad calls me Barbara. I wish Mom had insisted on Esperanza, but Dad said people would think he was Mexican if he had a kid named Esperanza.

My left foot was twisted inward. Mom pressed it out, trying to squeeze it into a normal shape.

"Her foot is fine, Simone," said Doctor Maclean, standing at her bedside. He wasn't tall, he wasn't good looking, his mouth was too thin, but he still affected her. "She was born the way God intended her to be."

He lifted Mom's hand from the foot.

"Has she fed yet?" he asked.

"She didn't seem to want the formula. Maybe I could try to give her my . . . you know . . . to feed her with . . ." She was too uncomfortable to say breast.

"Not until we've given you a transfusion. Our missionaries are giving blood now."

"I'm sorry, I . . ." She was about to apologize for hemorrhaging and mucking up the bedding.

"Breast feeding won't be very productive anyway, you both need to gain weight."

He pulled up a chair next to her bed.

"My dear," he started out, and Mom felt faint, the way she would when her father sat her down to ask why she went to her sister's concert barefoot or drilled a hole in the neighbor's boat. She preferred her mother's rages to her father's criticism.

"Do your parents know where you are?"

She was too anemic to lie. "My mom's not alive and my dad is—no, he doesn't."

"And is there a marriage certificate?"

She shook her head. "We wanted to save up for a wedding."

"I can't imagine you're saving much, judging from how often I see Jack going to the beer parlor when he's down here. Have you thought about your future, Simone?"

Mom's thoughts of the future got swallowed by the constant white fog that butted up against the landmass across the channel. Images from the past grew grotesque in her mind. Being with Jack had made the past disappear and the future not matter.

"The Nootka Mission has an extra cabin here."

A voice was singing loudly down the hall: "I had a hat when I came in and I'll have one when I go out!" Mom thought it was a dumb song with dumb words and a dumb melody, but Dad would spontaneously sing it from time to time and it made her laugh. He stood at the door with the three men he'd taken to breakfast. Not too drunk, just a little jolly.

"My friends here wanted to say hello to the baby. This is Oliver, Wesley, and Daniel."

The doctor stood guard over Mom's bed as the men filed in.

Randy came running into the room with Barb following behind him. Dad swooped him up and put him beside me. Randy cradled my face in his hands.

"Simone has to sleep," Doctor Maclean said. "The baby is too small for visitors." Nobody listened.

Oliver, Wesley, and Daniel viewed me from the other side of the bed and nodded to Mom. The fishy smell on their clothes was strong but it wasn't a rotten smell. It reminded her of fishing in a rowboat with her father. He always told her that Indigenous people were the best fishermen. They knew where the fish were.

Oliver stared at the details of Mom's face. He was full-blooded. Boils covered his cheeks and his black eyes were cloudy, but they had a calmness that made Mom feel safe.

If her mother were here, she thought, she'd be kissing everybody tearfully and cooing over *ma petite, ma belle petite*. Oliver would be telling her some special way to cook the clams she'd gathered on the beach. Dad would say something in French that had a double meaning and Lucille would laugh. For the first time in three years, Mom missed her mother.

"I think I have to sleep now," she said and closed her eyes.

Voices continued in her head for a cloudy moment or two.

"Do you have children, Oliver?" Barb asked.

"A girl, she's four and my boy's six. They go to the school in Tofino."

"Tofino? When the hell do you see them?"

"They come home at Christmas and for part of summer."

"They're at the residential school," Dad said, "learning to be white."

One morning there were hushed voices and hard-heeled shoes running down the hall. A man was shouting "How!?" and a nurse was sighing, "Oh dear, oh dear." Mom strained unsuccessfully to hear a whispered conversation between nurses outside her door. In the distance, Doctor Maclean was speaking to the man in tones too low to make out, but the man's words rang throughout the building: "How could a needle break?" he cried. "How?"

The nurses kept their voices down that day. Nothing was said about what happened and gradually Mom's curiosity gave way to exhaustion. She slept and forgot.

For the next week Mom went in and out of dreaming while the missionaries looked after Randy and me. Outside her window the rain was so thick she couldn't tell the difference between land, sea, and sky. The few times Dad visited they would whisk us babies away for baths, feeding, or naps. He was anxious to get his family out of there. After about ten days Mom was sufficiently fortified and going stir-crazy, but she had a new problem. Her thin ankles had ballooned to twice their size and her calves were bloated and misshapen. The head nurse told her not to worry. She wrapped Mom's lower legs in hot towels and elevated them.

Then the doctor said: "Venereal disease."

She was too embarrassed to ask him how venereal disease could make her legs swell. It didn't seem right, but she didn't dare question him, only cringed to imagine her father ever finding out.

"You know Jack has a past," Doctor Maclean said softly, resting his hand over Mom's hand. "Maybe you want to reconsider staying in one of our cabins."

At the Esperanza Hotel bar, Dad knocked back a shot of Scotch. He couldn't understand why the nurses were giving him the runaround. He'd tried to see Mom three times and they kept coming up with some bullshit excuse, like she was sleeping, or she was in with the doctor, or they weren't sure where she was. He'd always had a fondness for nurses but these women were sour and sanctimonious. They held onto his kids as if they were trying to shield them from him. The last time he'd gone back, a nurse at the front desk had given him a short note from Mom. All it said was: "I don't want to see you. Please stay away, Simone."

It didn't make sense, things were good between them. It was her writing, but Dad knew Doctor Maclean had put something in her head.

"Ah! These hands weren't made for holding butterflies," he mumbled, rubbing a gash on one of his knuckles, a memento from a close call with a chainsaw that morning. He'd send her money. He wasn't going to let these kids slip away. Not like the first ones. Dad had two daughters who were being raised by his parents. He had no contact with them, and he wasn't going to let that happen again.

Alcohol usually made him see the joke in his mistakes, but poured across this new wound it had him swearing out loud.

"No matter what, that bloody bible-thumping fraud is not going to baptize my children."

"Jack!" Mrs. Moore snapped, clearing empty glasses off the table.

Wesley and Oliver seconded his curses silently, knowing that if they raised their voices they'd be thrown out.

"By the way," she softened, "did you hear about the pregnant woman from Ceepeecee?"

"No, but there once was a pregnant nun from Anchorage," Jack jumped at the chance for some levity. "Do you know that one?"

"Doctor Maclean gave her a spinal block when she went into labor and the needle broke off."

"That's not too funny."

"She died."

Randy wrapped himself in a billowing sheet as Mom hung it on the line. It was a sunny day in November, the first time in a month it wasn't raining. Mom hoped the sun would stay long enough to dry the laundry. The fresh-air smell in her bedding reminded her of being back home in Jasper.

I was swaddled up in the carriage bawling and Randy was insisting Mom play peek-a-boo. Kids were fun but they were mostly work. At least here she didn't have to worry about Randy falling off the float house and drowning or getting crushed between the logs. The cabin was dry, she had a washing machine, she got food from the hospital, and the nurses held us kids sometimes, but she missed Jack. Reverend Maclean was right and kind, but Jack was fun. She was furious at him but that didn't take away her longing. She wished Dad could stay with us, but even if they married it wouldn't be allowed. Randy pulled down a wet sheet with him and rolled on the ground. Mom snatched it up and shook him out of it roughly. He saw it as a new game and tried to roll in the sheet again. In spite of her irritation, she couldn't resist his giggles, so she rolled him up and rolled him out one more time.

She thought she saw movement in the bush but she wasn't wearing her glasses and couldn't see at a distance. She walked closer, squinting. A scrawny cougar was standing on a low-lying stump, eyeing me, paying no attention to Mom. Its head was stretched forward and its limbs were slightly bent, ready to spring. Mom ran in front of the carriage and screamed, "Get!" The cat's head pulled back but its front legs were still poised to jump, ribs visible under a tawny hide that drooped below its hollowed abdomen. It was starving. It studied her, the obstacle to a life-saving meal. Mom twisted the wet sheet in her hand. The cougar turned its head toward another possible meal: Randy, who was running toward Mom still wanting to play their game.

Mom snapped the sheet and startled the cat. It snarled. Randy got between Mom's feet. The cat lurched to the side and skittered forward, trying to get around her, but she snapped her weapon inches from its face. It retreated then ran to the other side. She snapped at it again and screamed, "Get!" The cougar recoiled but then came forward ready to confront her. She snapped and snapped the sheet, screaming as loudly as she could. The cougar darted toward her between strikes, each time stunned back as the sheet hit its face again and again. Mom roared as she advanced, *snap snap snap*, whipping the beast with a ferocity she'd never felt before. The cougar gave one last growl then skulked away.

Mom picked Randy up and held him tightly. I'd gone silent with my eyes open wide, like an animal still in the circle of a predator's threat.

Reverend Maclean came running with his shotgun held at his chest. "Was it the cougar?" he asked.

The cougar had killed his dog and he'd frightened it off with a gunshot.

"Do you know how to use this?" He handed the shotgun to her. Mom didn't want a gun, she felt empowered by her victory, but the Reverend insisted, saying it would be irresponsible to her children not to have a gun.

Years later, she would reflect on the ugly feeling she got holding the dead steel.

The next day the Reverend Doctor shot the starving cougar as it crouched on top of a cabin.

Mrs. Moore set a steak in front of Dad. She offered him a complimentary tumbler of rum and eggnog, a little Christmas cheer, but Dad declined it. Tucked in his shirt pocket was a letter from Mom's dad. Most likely Doctor Maclean had tipped him off to her whereabouts. It wasn't good news for Dad, but he still wanted to be sober when he delivered it to her. She'd go back home he figured.

All day he worked in bone-cold December darkness, hands numb from gripping winch lines and whacking axes. He could justify a helluva lot of bad behavior for how hard he worked, but there wasn't a helluva lot of trouble to get into up there. The only women were taken or not taken for good reason. He had never had an interest in other women since he met Simone anyway. Now that she was out of his life he was a monk, with the exception of trips down the inlet to the hotel beer parlor.

In the corner he recognized one of his neighbors. It was Geordie, the guy who had thrown his baby's buggy onto the dock piling. He looked rougher than gravel on snow. "Geordie," he waved, "join me?"

Geordie raised his head and walked over. He sat looking glumly at the beer in his hand.

"So I hear it was a spark from a donkey engine that started

that fire in Tahsis." Dad tried to engage him. "Damn lucky the mill crew was there to stop it."

Geordie wasn't in a mood to talk.

"Christmas is a rotten time," Dad said, "no doubt about it."

"My boy," Geordie said quietly. "He's in the hospital." Then it spilled out of him.

"He had a sore on his arm. We figured it was a spider bite, he wasn't complaining too much, then this morning he woke up crying and the whole arm, right to his neck, was all puffed up."

"The poor little fella. They giving him penicillin? That seems to fix everything." Dad tried to be encouraging.

"The doctor says it has to come off."

"Well, that's not right. You've got to get a second opinion on that. I mean a man can go through life with one arm fine, but that seems a little extreme."

"They're getting him ready."

"Oh no. No, no," Dad said, pushing his plate away.

"Elaine, will you wrap up my steak?"

Jack and Geordie stood in the hospital reception area. No one was around. They heard a strange moaning sound and followed it down to the basement. "Like a bloody haunted house," Dad whispered.

Behind the cracked door the missionary nurses were lying on their stomachs, face down with arms over their heads, chanting. In front of them, Reverend Maclean was on his knees holding his head up to heaven incanting some non-sense. This was their prep for surgery.

Dad shook his head and pulled Geordie away. "Not gonna

happen," he said. Religion had cut too many things out of him before he was old enough to resist.

Upstairs, the four-year-old boy was lying sedated on a gurney, his swollen arm and half his torso painted with Mercurochrome. Dad moved in and lifted the boy into his arms. The nurse made little attempt to stop him.

Dad radioed a seaplane to Esperanza and they flew down to Port Alberni hospital. The doctor gave the boy a shot of penicillin and his arm was saved. The cost of the seaplane pretty much wiped out Dad's savings, but it just made him feel swell to be the hero, one hundred percent.

Since the gun came to the cabin, Mom felt less safe. It was too volatile. It made her think of her mother, who would just be sitting there quietly then suddenly go off. She'd break a wine glass, gash her wrist. Sometimes Lucille hurt herself, sometimes she hurt Mom, it was the same thing. Mom was the weakest, the youngest, the most attached, the one who drew on her mother's loneliness turned to anger, her love turned crazy. And the guilt, which made her do strange things. Mom hummed and jostled me around, trying to stop the thoughts conjured by the gun.

There was the story of the needle breaking in the woman's spine, and then one of the nurses casually asked Mom how her phlebitis was doing. She didn't know she had phlebitis. She looked up the word in a medical encyclopedia at the hospital library, the only non-religious book there. "Pregnant women face a particularly high risk for phlebitis—about one in one hundred newly delivered moms develops it—because pregnancy releases a tide of hormones that may effect the walls of the veins, usually in the legs." She read it over and over, scribbled down key words: pregnancy, hormones, swollen legs. There was no mention of venereal disease. Doctor Maclean had deceived her. All on a day when she was questioning his decision to leave my twisted foot as "the Good Lord intended it." She was terrified to confront him. She would rather fight a hungry cougar with a wet sheet.

So when Dad showed up with the letter from her father, Mom was relieved to escape.

Dad sat on the dock chewing the steak from two nights before. He was waiting for a boat down to Ceepeecee. They were paying double overtime for anyone who was willing to miss Santa Claus and endure the December wind on the western slope. He'd lifted a stack of *New Yorker* magazines from the hospital for nighttime reading.

Geordie's wife had invited Mom and us kids over for Christmas dinner. Dad was happy Mom wouldn't be alone. The kids were healthy. Simone had shown him some affection. She'd be in Jasper with her father by New Year's. Come spring, he'd get a job on the Alaska Pipeline that would put him on the mainland at least. He studied the impaled baby buggy, white tatters fluttering in neglect.

A Note on the Door

There is a small white rectangle on the front door of my mother's house. A note. I'm standing outside the gate, stunned but not surprised. The walkway, the road, the ferry, the last two days and my twenty-four years have all led me to this note. It's about my older brother, I know that.

It was raining hard but now the sun is out and I am shocked dry inside.

This house belonged to Dad's parents—after they died, his siblings donated it to him, I guess because he seems to be the most in need, but he doesn't want to own things. Sometimes he sleeps on the couch but not for very long. Even if he doesn't drink all night and burn holes in the furniture, he'll stay long enough to do something to aggravate my mother.

It's a sterile little box, neat, trim, and dark with repressed emotions. But something has been expressed. I know from where I stand outside the gate. I can feel the note being written by my mother's shaking hand, I can almost see the words.

I have the impulse to get back in my car and leave, but a voice stops me:

"Barbara."

A man is walking down a little path from the house next door.

"Have you spoken to your family?" he asks. I think his name is Mr. Scott. His head is cocked to one side and he's trying to appear sympathetic but he's too uncomfortable himself to be of any comfort.

"Would you like me to call your sister?"

I would never think to call my sister, not in a crisis. I'm the strong one, the big sister, the one people turn to. But I nod, "Sure."

It's sunny but I'm shivering. I press my body into the warm metal of my car and contemplate my few belongings strafed across the back seat. The day before, they were an anchor to some part of my life, now they are so much junk I would like to be rid of.

From the slight heat I'm sleepy. I could dump the stuff on the sidewalk, take a nap, and still catch the last ferry. I could deny my sixth sense and pretend the note is something else.

Mom would do that. She'd write something like, "Bye Barb, best of luck," and then not answer the door. She'd like to send me off with some encouragement, but she's just not versed in stuff like that. I could say I didn't see the note, or that I went to the wrong house, the wrong island, or I could just get out of here and not explain anything to anyone.

But I succumb and wait, resting against my Mazda until my sister is there, shaking like a wet cat on a limp branch. She's all sinew and bone.

Her boyfriend drives us to her apartment.

"Did you talk to Mr. Scott?" she asks. I guess she's wondering what he's told me.

"Not really. I wasn't sure that was him."

"He's gotten pretty fat." The way her mouth twists to one side, I wonder if she's on something.

"His wife's a complete tub. They're nice people though."

Marlene's spooky, she's so edgy.

Her boyfriend keeps snatching looks at me from the rearview mirror. He's seen me on stage and regards me as someone apart. I appreciate the boundary. I know I should ask what's going on but I just need to close my eyes.

I slip into a nowhere zone, like I'm inside a fuzzy TV set after the broadcasting has stopped. I think Randy is dead, but I can't be sure.

"Hi, Barb," I hear and eliminate all the places I'm not.

Mom is standing by the open car door, as pale as she's ever been. Her light-blue eyes are bloodshot. She's framed by baby-fine blond hair that shimmers against the sun. She's on the skinny side but she's beautiful. People always say she could have made money on her looks.

"Do you want some tea?" she asks.

I'm surprised she's not hiding in a dark room.

I step out of the car and my foot cramps. My old club foot. It's the barometer for my health. When I get run down and tired, the bones double up on each other.

Harry and Lucille

When he saw my odd gait, Granddad decided my foot had to be fixed. A surgeon said it would require operations, casts, braces, and a lot of money. Fortunately, the Shriners Club offered to pay for it. Unfortunately, Granddad refused to accept charity. He believed that we should never take hand-outs, and never take more than we need, since a person of character created their own resources. He used to send back the monthly checks the Canadian government doled out to all families because he was opposed to welfare.

He took me to another doctor who said he could fix me with braces alone. They were little shoes attached to a bar that could be adjusted every few months to direct my foot outward. I had to wear them all the time, so I was partly immobilized for a few years. I have a memory of being sick in my crib when I was a toddler. I was lying on my back trying to turn over because vomit was backing up in my throat. I cried out to Mom and banged my braces against the crib railing. But she didn't come. Mom tells me I banged

33

my braces against the crib every night until she could sleep through it. I was the girl who cried wolf. Then Mom never came when I really needed her.

It was fire season in the bush and we were staying with Granddad while Dad worked on the Alaska Pipeline. Mom was happy to get out of the coastal camps to dry out for a while. The weather in Jasper was crisp and mild. The roads were safe, no threatening trucks dominating the terrain. She could stroll with the babies. Everything was easier.

Granddad was outside having a cigarette before he went to sleep in the toolshed that was also his art studio. Mom could hear him coughing.

She was sleepy. She hoped she wasn't pregnant again. Her dad had been very firm about her not having more children. He didn't mention her deception, voiced no opinions about Jack, but his disappointment was palpable. She had to keep quiet about a letter she'd received that day. It would only add to Harry's concern. Dad wrote that he hated the Oklahoma contractors who were running the pipeline construction. He'd made a friend, a man the boss insisted enter the dining hall through a separate entrance because he was black. The man didn't seem to mind, but Dad thought it was complete bullshit, so he'd make a point by walking through the entrance with him. One morning, Dad was sitting in the crummy, just waiting for a drive to the worksite. His boss came up and said, "Get in the back of the crummy, boy." Dad replied that he was quite comfortable where he was and his boss repeated the order. Fortunately, Dad didn't knock his block off, instead he said "Fuck You" and quit. So now he was heading to Vancouver, looking for another job.

The house had not changed in the time she'd been gone. Every dish and towel, even Granddad's toothbrush, was the same. Harry was as frugal as he was lean. Waste was intolerable. Smoking was his one weakness, even though he emanated intelligence when he smoked. His lungs were damaged from inhaling mustard gas during the First World War. Her mother had told her that; he never spoke of the past. Her mother was one of the nurses who had tended to him after he was injured in the battle of the Somme, the same battle where her older brother was killed. Two years later, her other brother would die in the great flu epidemic.

At some point during the Second World War, Harry became a warden at a prisoner of war camp in Medicine Hat. Granddad thought conditions in the camps were quite decent, better than some of the barracks for Canadian soldiers. A few German prisoners who had escaped the camp came back, preferring to do logging and farming, rather than face grizzly bears in the wild. It was a comfortable transition for Granddad, being in an environment with structure and boundaries, but without the bloodiness of the battlefield. After the war, he became a forest ranger. When he wasn't working, he spent his time painting the peaks and lakes of the Rockies.

The coughing receded as he walked quickly out of range. The shed couldn't be good for his lungs either, with all that oil paint and turpentine.

Mom missed Dad, but she was in no hurry to leave her childhood home. She was lying on her sister Tinker's cot. Randy slept in her old bunk bed. The room was exactly the same, the same air-dried sheets and blanket, the same frayed rug on the floor, the same chipped white dresser with three drawers, now empty. The big difference in the house was the absence of smell. When her mother was alive, there was always the smell of cooking or canning or drying: strawberry jam in early summer, apple sauce in the fall, cloves and cinnamon, pumpkin pie, Thanksgiving turkey, Christmas cake, winter stews. With the first notion of spring, she would throw open all the windows and doors, wash every blanket and curtain, spank all the rugs, sweep away the dust, and scrub away all the lingering smells of the year before. She wasn't religious but she liked the ritual of Lent, and everyone was forced to fast on fresh spring air until the house was filled with the smell of baking bread.

They once lived in a big house in Ottawa but moved to this little house during the Depression. According to my grandmother Lucille, her family was rich when she was a young girl in France, but her father had abandoned them. Her mother and four siblings were forced to live in a one-room house with no plumbing in Dinard, a small village on the northern coast of Brittany. She said they were descended from an aristocratic family that was driven from their manor during the French Revolution and had changed their name from Derrien to Merrien. There is a spot down the coast from Dinard called Le Roche Derrien, which she claimed was named after her family. Lucille would have periodic spells of resentment, kicking doors and swearing in French, but they had nothing to do with her fallen status.

She got sad when Harry was away. And then her hands turned mean. Her moods became erratic and Mom grew afraid of her. She wanted to giggle with her mother about boys, ask her what she could and couldn't do with them, but instead her mom punished her for impulses she might be having. She pulled her hair, she shouted for no reason.

It was 1949, the end of a cold January in the Rockies when Mom and her parents took the train to Vancouver and checked into the Hotel Georgia. Lucille was seeing a doctor for her nerves. By the second day, her mood had already lifted. At lunch, she was speaking French with the waiter, laughing at his cute mispronunciations. Hotels and restaurants were a rare extravagance and she was loving it. She loved being served, but more than anything she loved her husband paying attention to her. Granddad suggested they all go next door to the Vancouver Art Gallery, but Lucille said she was going to take a nice luxurious bath and get her hair done at the hotel salon. Granddad didn't ask about the cost, anything was worth seeing Lucille happy again.

Mom returned to their room a few hours later, while Harry took a walk. She knew he was going to smoke a cigarette, but she wouldn't tell her mother. Lucille hated it when Harry smoked. Mom couldn't wait to bring her mom to the gallery the next morning—to show her the totem pole paintings of Emily Carr. The small room was dark when she arrived, except for a slice of light coming from behind the half-open bathroom door. The cot where Mom slept had been made up, but the covers on her parent's bed were rumpled on one side. Mom couldn't find the light. She called out for her mother and moved toward the bathroom. On the floor beside the bed, her mother was lying face-down. Mom knelt beside her and touched her face, it was cold. She hadn't gone to the hair salon. Mom pulled a blanket over her and waited for her dad to come.

The Suicide Show

In her small apartment, my sister Marlene sets down some tea. Her loyal blue budgie is stationed on her shoulder.

"How long have you lived here?"

The apartment is bare except for two stools at her kitchen counter and an oversized couch.

"Just a month. It's good. I get free rent for cleaning the building and there's a bus stop on the corner."

Dad is sunk into the couch, completely shined on something. He lifts his hand in a slow wave without looking up from his lap.

"It's close to the university, you should take some classes."

"In what?"

I shrug, not wanting to start a "so many opportunities" harangue. I take a cup of tea from Mom. Her hands are shaking.

"Jack," she says, offering Dad a cup, but he doesn't respond. "Jack," she says a little louder and kicks his foot.

"I'm here, I'm here." He comes to attention.

Her hands shake more as she thrusts the teacup at him.

"Thank you, Simone."

Dad grips the cup, slips a cigarette in his mouth and moves toward the balcony.

Marlene shouts, "Don't open the door!" She shelters her budgie.

Dad nods, "Yup, yup, gotcha. You stay there, Max," he says, making a growling dog-face at the bird, then spills tea on the carpet as he jerks the door shut.

"I'll get that." Mom fetches a rag.

"I'll do it," says Marlene, getting down on her hands and knees. The tableau of the two of them scrubbing up Dad's mess makes me claustrophobic. I step around and go out to the balcony.

"You doing that *18 Wheels* play back East?" asks Dad.

"No. It's a Lillian Hellman play."

Under the influence, Dad's lips seem to expand and his otherwise dignified face takes on a goofy look.

"No music then."

"No, it's called *Toys in the Attic.* Do you know it? It's autobiographical."

"About when she was blacklisted?"

"When she was younger . . ."

"Oh. Too bad."

I think Dad enjoys seeing me in plays. He's never shown up drunk. Last time he came directly from the boats with a duffel bag full of oysters on ice, all the way from Alaska. He fried them up in the green room kitchen after the show and the whole company thought he was exceptionally cool.

"Nothing could be worse than that St. Joan of the Stock-yards thing. What a turgid bore that was. I like Brecht's politics but his plays are dreary. I'd rather see you in Shaw's *Saint Joan*. It's got more life in it."

Dad has knowledge about things you wouldn't expect. He's not what you'd call cultured but he reads a lot. His friends range from illiterate whistle punks to prize-winning poets.

"I'm supposed to start rehearsals tomorrow, but it doesn't look like I'm going to get there." I look at him, hoping for a moment he'll talk about what's happened, or at least say something meaningful.

He purses his lips and stares blankly at the stucco wall of the apartment building next door.

"I liked *18 Wheels*. You had some nice songs in that." He lights the Export Plain dangling from his mouth and the anchor tattoo on his forearm turns upright. He takes a deep long drag. I have a huge urge to ask for one, but I don't want him to know I smoke. In one of his abstinent spells, he had said that anyone who smokes is a fool. I'd like him to think I listen when he makes sense.

"Were you there, Dad?"

"We were coming down the inner channel last night and a boom got snagged up around Nanaimo, so I slept on the boat."

He keeps staring at the blank wall, puffing on the smoke.

"So you weren't there?"

Dad signals the alarm to change the subject by growling in the back of his throat. He's been around a lot of death and talks about it freely, but this is too close. He'll go into great detail about some guys who underestimated the power of a rip current or who tied the wrong knot when their life depended on it. "Pete Simpson, had no right to be up a spar tree, let alone to take a pee off one," he'd say. "But there he was, eighty feet high. He must have tripped on the lead line, it popped right out of the rigging block. We carried him out of the bush in my duffle bag. That was a real suicide show."

That's what they called the dangerous operations, suicide shows. I used to ask him before he left for camp if it was going to be a suicide show. When we lived in camp with him, I saw him strapped in stretchers more than a few times. Once he was being held upright because he couldn't breathe lying down. That was after he'd fallen from a loader, and he thought his heart had stopped. As soon as he got his wind back, he was asking for a cigarette.

Dad works on tugboats now, but as a logger he'd been a choke setter, a high topper, a rigger, and a boom man, but the job that always stuck in my head was a faller, because he fell so often.

One time he was rigging a spar tree and somehow got shook loose when he lopped the top off. He didn't cinch the flip-line or something like that. He fell about thirty feet before a single branch that he'd decided to leave broke his fall, then he bounced another twenty feet to the ground. He was badly banged up. That's probably when he broke his back but he's not sure.

I remember flying in a helicopter above a white rectangle in a deep green forest. The rectangle was the stretcher Dad was lying on. Over the sound of the chopper, Mom was shouting with Dad's boss, Ivan Pretty. She wasn't wearing her glasses because Mr. Pretty was handsome. Dad called him pretty Mr. Pretty.

As we approached the ground I got dizzy. I willed myself not to throw up. When the door opened, the chopper was louder. My insides rattled. Only the smell of cedar pitch and sawdust grounded me.

The only color in Dad's face was the dried blood at the sides of his mouth and under his nose. He was too weak to grit his teeth. There were streaks running from his eyes through the mask of grime.

Mom looked vexed. I imagine she was wondering how long he was going to be laid up. This was before government health care. Hospitals were expensive—we'd have to move back into one of the smaller houses in the camp. She hated those houses, they barely had any windows and were too close to the garbage dump. You had bears coming to the back porch and skunks in the crawl space. Her father was coming to visit and she didn't want him to be sleeping in a cubbyhole of a living room. They'd moved twenty times and she was finally in a decent two-bedroom house, then Dad had to blow it with another accident.

Randy squeezed between the workers hoisting Dad to the medics and stood on tiptoes trying to see him. Dad lifted his hand. His fingers were always bent, ready to haul a winch line or to grip an axe, oil and dirt embedded in every crack. The men's shouts were blurred by the noise of the helicopter. They all had dirty hands, stubbly beards, and sweaty faces. Some were missing fingers. Most of them looked familiar from the camp cookhouse, where we sometimes ate pancakes on Sunday mornings. Some were bare-chested under their suspenders, though it wasn't warm.

Dad was scowling, I don't think from the pain but because he hated us seeing him weak. This was his arena, where he proved himself, made up for all his weaknesses in civilian life. Finally Mom walked up and put a lit cigarette in his mouth.

Bear Creek

My fifteen-year-old brother Bobby arrives at Marlene's with his friend. They look like basketball players. Bobby's six-two and his friend's even taller, wholesome island teenagers. Bobby's head is bowed and his face is stricken with a sadness that makes grief not ugly. He hugs me and rests his head on my head. "I can't believe it, it's just not real," he says.

I don't know Bobby well, he was five when I left home. He favors Mom, silver-blue eyes and blondish. Usually when I see him he's flushed and full of oxygen from kicking or throwing some kind of ball. Randy was athletic too, but Bobby is stable. Mom had pretty much expelled Dad from the house when she moved to the island. That made life a lot more stable.

His friend hunches down to my level. "I'm really sorry," he says, with blue eyes that hide nothing.

I feel claustrophobic again and start to open the balcony door.

"No!" Marlene shouts.

I wonder how we should move things forward. Isn't there a body somewhere, waiting to be delivered?

The phone rings. Marlene answers with a dry whisper. Her eyes roll. She says, "It's Misty."

Misty is Dad's daughter from his first marriage, our step-sister and the scapegoat for many familial ills. She lives off the grid in a float house on one of the Gulf Islands. Misty's not her real name. She reinvents herself every few years.

Mom sighs.

"Not the time to be holding onto grudges, Simone," Dad says.

"Ya." Marlene's mouth squirms about as she listens to Misty on the phone, "Ya ya . . . Uh huh."

"Can you pick her up at the bus depot?" Marlene asks me.

I shake my head no.

"I'll get her," Dad says.

"No Dad, you won't." Bobby steps in. His mental health is a thing of wonder to me. So many times I've left my body in fear while Dad drove smashed out of his gourd, narrowly missing head-on collisions, cruising over lawns, around tele-phone poles, startling dogs, and jumping ditches. Ironically, I only ever got injured in a sober car accident when Mom was driving. She rounded a corner and the passenger door flew open while I was holding baby Kate on my lap. She wasn't going very fast, it was a faulty door. I rolled out on the pave-ment, cradling Kate. I got a monster bruise on my elbow and nasty abrasions on my cheek, but I was a hero for protecting the baby.

Marlene's boyfriend volunteers to drive and Marlene comes

along. I don't know how Misty makes a living but she always has pot. I suspect that's why Marlene is eager to see her.

In spite of the pain in my foot or maybe because of it, I feel the need to go running. I ask Marlene and her boyfriend to drop me at my car.

As I'm going out the door, Mom comes over and hands me a tattered Purdy's chocolate box held together by tape. I haven't seen it for years. I'm surprised it has survived the rain pummeling our evicted possessions on the front lawns of locked houses, the midnight escapes from unpaid motel rooms, and, above all, the careless generosity of Dad, who always had to give some special gift to an interesting new acquaintance.

The box holds all our family photographs.

"Maybe you could take care of this," Mom says.

I'm not exactly sure what she means.

The note is still on the door.

It's a portent, a crack between everything that was and what comes next. I must endure the crack and not be swallowed by it.

I should go inside and call the theater in Toronto and tell them I've been delayed by a family emergency but I'm not prepared to say anything yet.

I have a pair of shorts and shoes, which I change into inside my car. My car feels like a can of dead things now. I open the chocolate box and the first picture is one I don't recognize. It's Randy and me in front of a fireplace holding toys.

We're in Granddad's house. On the mantle I see the oil painting and brass candlestick holders we inherited after he died. This is pre-braces, my foot turns in.

We moved every few months when we were little, which I have no memory of, but Mom is always mentioning this-and-that place we lived while we waited for or followed Dad's next job.

The first place I remember, and the last place Dad lived with us full-time, was Bear Creek. I was five. All the pictures we have are from when Granddad came to visit, since we never owned a camera.

I adored Granddad. I loved his English accent, so elevated in the rough world of loggers. I loved how meticulous and neat he was, how he explained things so clearly. He made a worksheet of impeccably drawn numbers and letters for us to practice copying every night after dinner. Before bed he would slather polish on his shoes and set them on the outside steps. In the morning he would buff them up to a high shine. He taught us how to fold our clothes and make our beds, military-style. He wasn't affectionate, but he was responsible and organized. I can see him in front of me, gripping his Brownie camera, waiting for the right moment, his sleeveless white T-shirt showing his sculpted arms. I have arms like his. He's wearing his shiny old blood-leather shoes. His face is strong and graceful, chiseled to the bone. His eyes are pale blue like Mom's. He has a furrowed brow and serious expression, not troubled or heavy, just impatient with weakness in himself or other people.

Here I am at the playground in Bear Creek. From that swing I could see all the houses and the main hall, which was also the schoolhouse, church, and bingo hall. I could see the logging trucks carrying their loads down to the booming ground. I could see the kids coming home from school, neighbors visiting neighbors, and Mr. Pretty's pickup truck bringing supplies to the commissary and cookhouse. The playground was the center of everything.

In the summertime, Mom put lemon in my hair and butter on my skin. My left leg is still shy from wearing braces here. After they were removed, I had to wear my shoes on the opposite feet to make them grow straight. I wonder if I always crossed my legs to make it look like my feet matched.

Our house is behind me, surrounded by tall thistles and weeds butting up against the thick dark forest. There's an empty clothesline stretching out from the back porch, where I once jumped so hard a jar of kerosene fell from a shelf and cut my head open.

Debbie Shankervelt lived next door. We tried to make dandelion wine together. Maybe we heard it in a song. I didn't know wine was alcohol. To me, alcohol was beer and Scotch, because that's what Dad drank.

We filled a giant bowl from Debbie's kitchen with dandelions and carried it upstairs to the attic, where we ripped open a fifty-pound bag of sugar, letting it spill over the floor. We mashed the white grains into the yellow heads with wooden spoons, expecting the mush to liquefy.

Suddenly Debbie was yanked up by her hair and hit in the face.

"What the hell is this?" her mother screamed, hitting her again, then kicking her in the back with a viciousness I'd never seen. I scrambled out of there and barricaded myself under my bed.

Lying awake that night, I came up with a plan to rescue Debbie from the hands of her mother. I took some wooden matches from the kitchen drawer and a stack of newspaper from the back porch and snuck over to her house.

I called to Debbie and she appeared at the window.

"Come outside," I whispered.

In spite of my dread of encountering a skunk or some other creature under the house, I slithered through a hole into the crawl space. All I felt was moist ground, I couldn't see. I gripped the head of two matches, the way Randy had showed me, and struck them against each other. A flame illuminated my hands and just as I was igniting the newspaper, something gripped my ankles. In one motion I was whooshed out and dangled upside down. My Dad walloped me twice on my backside, uprighted me, and shoved me in the direction home.

Debbie disappeared from the window. Nothing was said. It was the only time in my life Dad hit me.

One day Randy was riding his bike on the road and saw Debbie's brother chop her finger off. She wouldn't take her finger away from the chopping block when Ricky was chopping wood, so he chopped it. Randy said she didn't cry, she just stared at the blood coming out. Ricky ran into the bush.

Randy yelled for Mrs. Shankervelt and she carried Debbie

down to the commissary. The doctor told Randy to hurry back and get the finger but when he got there it was gone. Maybe an animal took it, maybe Ricky.

Next to the Shankervelts was Mr. Russell's house. I don't know if the Russells had children somewhere. He was an old man, I think he was an engineer or something that didn't require strength. He was handy with machinery and stuff and was always giving me little things he invented. He cut swaths of pictures from magazines and glued them on the blades of an electric fan. When he turned it on, it was a whirling kaleidoscope of changing shapes and merging colors. I'd never seen anything like it. His wife was in a wheelchair and couldn't see anything because she was blind from cataracts. Mr. Russell used to be my friend, but years later I would realize he was a sick person.

I remember Randy and me hanging upside down on the monkey bars in Bear Creek, tracking Mario the cook as he sprinted behind the single row of houses, carrying a rifle. He ran up the front stairs of our house and started bellowing like a moose. Mom didn't open the door.

We jumped down and approached the house. It wasn't uncommon to see people with rifles in Bear Creek—there were wild animals to contend with—but an angry man with a loaded gun on our front porch was new.

Mario walked down the stairs staring straight ahead, looking right through us. Then he walked around the side of the house, cocking his gun. Mom cracked the front door and peered out holding baby Marlene. Randy pointed to the side of the house where Mario had gone and suddenly a woman I can't remember ever seeing before crept out from behind Mom and rushed over to the next house, where she flattened herself against the side wall.

There was a crashing of glass from the back porch, then the Moose was bellowing from inside our house.

"She's not here!" Mom yelled at him. She motioned for us to go away but we stayed.

Mario burst through the front door and Mom didn't flinch, she just rocked the baby up and down. Mario was waving his arms, the way he did when he got mad in the cookhouse one time, and Mom had said he had a temper because he was Italian. I couldn't understand anything he was shouting.

Mom sat down on the steps and when Mario's back was turned she mouthed, "Get Dad."

Randy turned quickly and Mario, sensing the movement, spun around with his rifle pointed right at him. Mom screamed. Everyone froze and the baby started crying.

Mario's face got all rubbery, he shook his head side-to-side and dropped to the ground beside Mom. Randy took off to the boathouse, where Dad was working on his boat. The mysterious woman was still hiding beside the neighbor's house. I was afraid to look in case Mario saw me do it.

"Go get a bottle for the baby," Mom said, and I squeezed past her and Mario.

There was glass on the kitchen floor from the broken backdoor window. Then Dad and Jim Martindale came whispering through the house, Dad motioning for me to stay back.

There were some shouts, sounds of struggle, then Mom

came racing in, handed me the baby, and got a roll of twine from the back porch.

Mario was tied up and kept bellowing until the RCMP came over on a speedboat from Harrison and took him away.

Dad put a piece of plywood over the broken backdoor window and we never saw Mario again.

Behind our next house, Randy and I made a path through the forest to the creek. There was a clearing that allowed a bit of sunlight. It was a damp place thick with ferns and moss and bugs under rocks. It's where I first saw crocuses in spring.

Mom didn't like us going alone because of cougars and bears, but we would sneak down and play for hours, hopping from rock to rock across the creek, trying not to get wet. She would be yelling for us, but had no idea where our trail was.

Once I offered to take the baby for a walk, happy to give Mom a break. She told me to keep to the side of the road but I forgot and meandered into the middle. I was singing to myself—deep in song—when a loud blast broke my reverie. A monster logging truck with wheels taller than me was a few feet from my heels. The driver leaned his whole torso out the cab window and yelled: "Get the hell out of the way!" I was frozen in shock, then Marlene started bawling. The driver gave two more blasts of his horn and Marlene bawled louder.

I got to the side of the road and jiggled the buggy, trying to shush her, but she screamed even louder than the truck's horn. I didn't know how to calm her. I felt like I'd done something terrible and I couldn't bring her home in this state. I worried people in the neighborhood might think I'd hurt her. So I bumped the screaming baby down our secret path to the creek.

I found a level bit of ground and parked her there. The change of scenery seemed to make her curious and she shut up for a second. It was a little chilly under the trees by the water because it was starting to get dark. I thought maybe she had smartened up and we could go home now, so I backed up the buggy, but then she started wailing worse than before. I don't understand why, but I ran away. I left the baby in her buggy by the creek.

When I got home Mom was in the kitchen making dinner, so I dashed into my bedroom without saying a word. I sat on my bed with the kaleidoscope fan that Mr. Russell had made for me, spinning it with my fingers. Several minutes passed and I thought maybe I was off the hook, but then the door opened. Mom glanced around the room, looking puzzled more than anything else.

"Where's Marlene?"

I twirled the fan faster, trying to think of a good answer.

Mom sat on the edge of my bed and put her hand on the fan to stop its spinning.

"Barbara," she lifted my chin forcing my eyes to meet hers, "where is the baby?"

She wasn't mad. She had that "I'm not going to hurt you, just tell me" tone.

I told her, "By the creek." And she said, "Where? Where by the creek?"

Randy was standing with us now so I looked over to him.

"I know where," he said.

Randy led Mom down the path with a flashlight and they found the baby sleeping peacefully.

Mom didn't punish me. She was never big on punishment.

In Bear Creek, there was a boy named Dennis Beazle whom Mom took pity on because she thought he was being abused by his parents. I heard Dad say the parents were blood cousins and that's why Dennis wasn't right in the head. I never saw his father but his mother was old and mean-looking.

Dennis had a younger brother who came to school, but Dennis stayed home. He crouched on a rotted stump at the corner of his yard beside the schoolhouse. His hair was shaved close to his head, his ears stuck out, and his forehead was wrinkled. With his knees next to his ears, he looked like a monkey. He would pounce to the ground holding his penis out and chase after Debbie and me, trying to pee on us.

One night Randy found our cat, Puff, lying on the back porch unable to move and wheezing. Her once-fluffy white coat was covered in thick, black grease. When we tried to lift her she lamely clawed and snarled. She had puncture wounds on her back.

Dad restrained her while Mom washed her in a soapy bath.

One of our neighbors found their cat dead beside an open oil barrel, and it was determined that the Beazle boy had forced the cats in then stabbed at them with a hunting knife.

Mom went to talk to the parents.

"Did he do it?" I asked when Mom came home.

"Yes, but it's not his fault."

That made no sense and I wished someone would stick Dennis in a barrel of oil and poke him with a knife to see how he liked it.

Late at night, I heard Mom whispering to Dad. "You can't believe it, Jack. That poor boy. She pressed his hands against a red-hot stove. I saw it. He has blisters in the shape of the stove's element."

Puff lost all her hair and got so skinny that she looked like a shriveled little monster. She slept on top of the radio all the time and sometimes I thought she might be dead, but then I'd hear her crunching the kibble in her bowl. When she recovered, her hair grew back even fluffier than before. Dennis still crouched on the stump, looking like a shriveled little monster too, but he didn't dare chase me anymore.

This is Randy on his first day of school, standing on the steps of our little schoolhouse with Bobby and Jeannie Clark. Classes went to grade seven, with most of the kids on the younger side, about fourteen kids total in one common room. I was in kindergarten with Debbie Shankervelt and Darlene Martindale.

It was on those steps, right where Randy is standing, that I was sitting and looking at a book one day when suddenly I understood a word: "Spot." Spot was a dog, we'd learned that. "See Spot Jump." I knew he was jumping. "See Dick run." Dick was a boy. He was running and jumping with Spot. The words all brought images to me. The day before, they were just a frustrating jumble of letters and now they all made sense. I was reading! I breezed through that book and couldn't wait to read another one. I thought of how Dad was always reading when he was home. Now I could.

Bobby and Jeannie are twins, probably eight years old. Randy's pencil case is a Cut-Rite wax paper box. Our pencil cases were always wax paper boxes. Randy's look of being uncomfortable with himself is set right there.

Bobby and Jeannie lived in a neatly painted blue and

white house, with a green grassy lawn and white fence. Our house was paintless, with a yard of dirt and crabgrass. Bobby once declared a black and orange caterpillar was his, so I stepped on it to prove no one could own a caterpillar. Then he impaled the creature on the end of a stick and jammed it in my eye. Randy pummeled him, even though Bobby was a head taller, and Bobby went home whimpering. I ran home screaming that I had a "helicopter" in my eye.

At the first-aid clinic in the back of the commissary they had to freeze my eyeball to pull out the quills with tweezers.

Bobby's mom, Mrs. Clark, came over with Revellos, chocolate covered ice cream bars that were a rare treat in the camp. Randy sat on his twin bed glowering at the bar in his lap. No way would he eat the peace offering. I was tempted.

"Now, I know Bobby shouldn't have done that, but you stepped on his caterpillar, Barbara, and Randy you had no right to hit him."

Randy eyed Mrs. Clark with hostility as she walked out. I threw my melting ice cream bar at her and it smeared down her back.

She shrieked and waved her finger at my mom. "Are you going to do something about that, Simone?"

Mom stepped up and pushed me back into our room. She grabbed a pillow and walloped it, then mouthed for me to scream.

"Ow!" I cried, catching on.

"Don't you ever do that again!" she yelled, thumping some more.

"I'm sorry." I pretended to cry.

Mom was cool. She taught a tap dance class in the main hall once a week after dinner. About eight housewives in pedal pushers would huff and puff as they tried to follow her amid bawling babies and unruly kids. I don't know if Mom was qualified to teach, but she had such beautiful long legs, any-which-way she moved was a joy to watch.

I couldn't trust my foot to land where I wanted, so I found my footing in Sabbath school. I learned that God was a magical being watching us from somewhere in the sky, who would bless us with happiness and gifts for being good. He was kind of like Santa Claus, whom I once had great hopes for, but who let me down when I sat on his lap and he reeked of booze.

I don't know how The Seventh Day Adventists got the license to be the only church in town. Sabbath school was mainly appreciated by the parents as a daycare service. The teacher was Darlene Martindale's mother. She was dumpy and deceptively mild, and she was married to Jim, Dad's best drinking buddy in the camp.

In sight of parents, Mrs. Martindale would smile and pat our heads, but when the doors closed she filled our little heads with frightening scenarios. She got me believing that Mom's dancing and lipstick, along with Dad's many sins, would keep them out of heaven. On the day of the Second Coming, God would descend on a big cloud and all the good people would get on board. Dead people who had lived righteous lives were in a soul sleep and would wake up to join the good people ascending to heaven. Sinners would run in fear and perish. I knew Dad would never run, he wasn't afraid of anything. He would probably tease God for wearing a dress, just before he got consumed in flames.

I started to live in fear of clouds. If one seemed to be coming closer I'd convince myself I could hear the strains of trumpets. I'd drop to my knees, begging God to please let my whole family get on board. It was unbearable to think that some of us would make it and some not.

Mrs. Martindale told us we should only eat vegetables, but

a little bit of meat was acceptable as long as we ate God's chosen animals.

"And what would those animals be?" she asked.

Cows, chickens, and turkeys.

Dad had recently shot a bear and it was our winter supply of meat, so I piped up with "bear."

"Oh no, we don't eat bear, that's not one of the animals God chose."

Dad shot the bear because it was following us to school. We heard the shot right behind us. Then a second blast to finish it off. It was skinned and butchered by the time we came home. Dad hung the thick black hide on the back porch. There was no being finicky at the kitchen table, food was never wasted. But now I had a spiritual dilemma.

At every meal, I started shoving my bear meat behind a loose wall panel next to the kitchen table, and I prayed harder.

Mom was sure a rat had died somewhere between the walls and pulled the panels off, uncovering my stash of rotting carcass. If I'd known about trichinosis in bear meat I would have used that as my defense. I couldn't bring myself to tell Mom that she was forcing me to burn in hell with her, so I feigned ignorance.

On the porch, the bear hide got rained on and the skin part grew slimy. I'd shut my eyes and run down the stairs when I went past it. Mom told Dad to get rid of it, but he insisted he was going to turn it into a nice furry rug for the living room. Then the hide started sprouting mold and looked like it had a grotesque disease. When the sun came out, the stench bloomed and no one would go out the back door anymore. Mom finally screamed at Dad and he carried it down to the dump.

I tried to convince Randy to come with me to Sabbath school. How fun would it be to bounce on God's endless cloud together? But he said he'd stick with Mom and Dad.

Behind the main hall was a logging road that went past the garbage dump. One of our more exciting activities was to drive up with Mr. Pretty and watch the bears take garbage right off the back of his pickup truck. Then he'd lurch the truck back and forth to shake the bears off.

Down by the water in Bear Creek were the booming grounds. Kids weren't allowed on worksites, but as long as Mr. Pretty wasn't around no one said anything. I had seen a TV show called *Have Gun Will Travel* at Debbie Shankervelt's house and became convinced that one of Dad's co-workers was the main character, Paladin. Television was taboo with the Seventh Day Adventists, but it was too alluring for me to resist. Paladin had a thick black moustache and wore a black cowboy hat on the show and on the booms. It made me feel so special that he was working with my Dad. When I knew Mr. Pretty wasn't on site, I'd sneak down and look for Paladin.

On booming grounds, stripped trees roll off big trucks and slowly crash into the water, causing a ripple effect through the flanks of the boomed logs. The boom men ride out the swell then capture the loose logs and chain them together into booms. Then the booms are towed to the sawmills. It took skill to stay balanced on the rolling logs; it wasn't grunt work at all. Dad was fast and agile, jumping from log to log, always with an Export Plain hanging out of his mouth. When Dad saw me, he'd sing out the opening bars of the theme song to *Have Gun Will Travel*, "Paladin, Paladin, oh where do you roam?" Paladin would turn around and wave his hat at me and I'd picture him galloping across the plains.

If you followed the shoreline to the right you'd come to the swimming beach, my favorite place, even though I couldn't swim. I had a fear of putting my head under water. There was a man-made breakwater that sheltered the beach and kept us from the outside world. A lot of the escaped logs from the booming grounds settled here. Some were still floating, others were banked in the sand, all bleached out. Randy would slither in the water and under the logs like a minnow while I gripped the side of a log and kicked my feet until my lips turned blue from the cold. The water was glacial, but we had nothing to compare it to. The best part was playing on the logs, trying not to fall, then burrowing into the warm white sand.

One day Ivan Pretty was driving by the beach and spied a cougar checking out us kids. His .22 was within easy reach and he took the cougar down in one shot. We didn't know where the shot came from until we saw Mr. Pretty lifting the big cat into the back of his pick-up truck. We ran over all google-eyed. Mr. Pretty told us we shouldn't be at the beach alone and he let us ride in the back with the cat. I'd never seen a cougar up close. It had yellow-green eyes that were still open, like it was thinking. Its eyes were outlined by black markings that went down the side of its nose and around its white muzzle. It had such a beautiful face I started to feel sad for it. Just when I was mustering the nerve to pet it, the truck rounded a corner and the cat's front paw slapped Randy's foot. We both shrieked. I almost jumped out of the truck.

The dock was probably the most important fixture in Bear Creek. It's where Dad launched the speedboat he'd built—the Barlene, named after us girls, Barbara and Marlene. It was a proud day with picnics and a lot of beer. It seemed the whole town was watching as Dad and Jim Martindale putted past the breakwater, then spun out into the lake. Randy and I stood on a stump trying to see over the spectators. Dad was bombing through the water at high speed, showing off, doing figure-eights. People were oohing and ahhing and laughing as the boat did sharp turns and Jim and Dad got soaked in spray. Suddenly the boat stopped and everybody stood in silence, waiting for the next feat. But nothing happened. Someone said, "Must be a beer break," and we all kept waiting.

Then someone else said, "They're coming back." The boat hardly seemed to be moving but after a long time it rounded the breakwater. As it neared the dock, you could see that Dad and Jim were paddling with their lifejackets. The motor had dropped off.

Later in the week, someone with a scuba tank retrieved the motor. It was laid out on the dock and the diver said, "It's pretty jammed up, Jack," and I wondered what kind of jam coated the bottom of Harrison Lake.

The dock was also where the Tarquin, a converted tugboat that served as our ferry to civilization, came and went. Dad had gone to Chilliwack and promised to bring back a TV the next day. I had developed an obsession with television. TV joined me to a world that was so much bigger than my own. I watched

I Love Lucy, Have Gun Will Travel, Popeye, and *Tarzan.* I liked Paladin but I loved Tarzan. When I asked Dad why Tarzan never came to Bear Creek, he said, "Cause he's afraid of me."

Randy and I stood waiting as the Tarquin sputtered up to her berth.

After all the families hauled away their groceries and new appliances, Dad emerged from the cabin with nothing but bleary eyes.

"Where's the TV?" I asked, but I already knew.

Dad just mumbled and staggered past us.

"You promised you'd buy a TV."

"Well, you promised you'd learn to swim."

Dad was always trying to get me to dunk my head in the water, maybe that's why I had such a phobia about it.

"I can swim," I whispered.

"Ya? Let's see. Let's see you swim."

The sun had set and the water was black.

"Not now."

"No time like now," he said, picking me up by the scruff of my shirt and the waist of my pants and tossing me through the air into the shock of cold blackness. I didn't know which side was up, but my face found the surface and I gasped for air.

"Dig like a dog!" he shouted. "Dig like a dog!"

I dug frantically, barely keeping my nose above the water.

Dad yelled something again.

"What?" I cried and took in a mouthful.

"Get your feet behind you. Put your face down and get your feet behind you!"

I was sinking and choking, and all I could do was follow Dad's instructions. I took a breath and put my face into the unknown and started kicking. Digging and kicking. When I couldn't stand it anymore I lifted my head and sucked in air. Randy was wading in from the shore and I propelled myself toward him, not to Dad even though he was closer.

I spewed, kicked, and dug, and only when Randy was beside me holding my shoulders, did I release my feet to the bottom. It didn't feel like jam at all. Randy held my hand and we slogged our way to shore.

Dad came sniggering down the dock, "Well, now you can swim."

I was shaken but I also felt an incredible satisfaction. I would never be afraid of the water again. But I wasn't about to let Dad think he'd done me a favor. Randy and I walked ahead of him, shivering in our wet clothes, ignoring him all the way home.

Sunshine on bleached logs, green water reflecting endless forest. This is the last picture Granddad took of us in Bear Creek. There's my left foot, still hiding behind the right.

On his last day Granddad took us fishing off the breakwater. I remember my feet dangling high above the water and little minnows nibbling on the worm at the end of my line that hung from a stick. I was more interested in feeding fish than catching them.

"You're talking to yourself," Granddad said.

He always got annoyed when I talked to myself.

Randy was using Granddad's fishing rod and landed a fish with almost no help. I winced when Granddad slapped its head on a rock. They caught a few more and we brought them home for dinner.

I forced down a few mouthfuls of their catch as Granddad praised Randy. To shift the attention my way, I did a little faux tap dance, demonstrating how well my foot had healed.

I was stalling bedtime, trying to savor every minute of Granddad's last night. I suggested dessert, but Mom said there wasn't any. I was sure there was a tin of pears so I started rummaging. In the camps, supplies came industrial-sized. Cans were twelve-inches high and eight inches round. I pulled out what I thought was a can of pears but it was corn niblets. "Shoot," I said and then *thunk* it dropped on my foot. My freshly fixed foot. Dad was sitting at the table shaking his head. Mom looked like she might be sick. I was screaming. I still remember the shock of pain.

Then I smelled Ivory soap. My face was wet against Granddad's scrubbed neck. "Oh my poor little lamb." His voice was so close and tender, it was almost worth the pain.

Beyond the Breakwater

I don't remember anything more about Bear Creek after Granddad left. We moved to Harrison Hot Springs. Granddad wrote me a long letter in his gorgeous calligraphy asking how I liked our new home. It took me weeks to write him back, copying the curves and flow of each letter, especially the curled tail of the G in Granddad.

I told him Mom had a new baby, Dad was going to be away for a long time to work in a camp, I had no friends, and please come see us soon.

In my attic bedroom I discovered I could remove part of the wall and disappear into a crawl space. It was utterly black, kind of claustrophobic, but also exciting. I fetched some matches from downstairs and lit them to illuminate the passage. It was only high enough for me to crawl or sit and went all the way to my brother's room, where I discovered another removable patch in the wall. I kept it secret from everyone. If Mom was calling me, I would close the wall and sit in the dark silence. When the flame from a match no longer seemed bright enough, I started hoarding bundles of newspaper to crumple up and light. Once a support beam started burning and I extinguished it by frantically banging the flames with rolled-up newspapers. Sometime after that, Mom followed her nose upstairs and asked me if I'd been playing with matches. I didn't admit to anything but Mom made me feel guilty by telling me the horrors of what might happen if our house caught fire.

"Say if the baby was in her crib and the flames blocked us from getting to her," she said.

I realized how scary it was to be a mother. Not only did she have to feed and clothe us, she had to make sure nothing terrible happened to us. That night I gathered up all my dolls and placed them across the top of my bed side-by-side and tucked them in. My Inuk doll went in the middle. I said a little prayer for them to always be safe and happy, then I made a bed of jackets on the floor and slept there. I dreamed I was trying to dress my Inuk doll but she kept growing bigger and bigger and the dress kept getting smaller. Then the dress started growing and my doll got smaller and smaller until she disappeared. It became a recurring nightmare.

We were at a real school now but we couldn't make any friends. To keep us together, they held Randy back a grade, which was humiliating for him. He spent most of his time in the school library to avoid everyone. Mom started avoiding contact with people too. I thought if people met my pretty mom they'd want their kids to play with us, but Dad was more likely to be introducing himself with a case of beer.

Dad came back from camp just when it was time for parent-teacher meetings. We wanted Mom to go but Dad was keen to say hello to our teacher, Miss Bailey. Randy and I scrambled behind him, pleading for him not to go. He'd grown a beard, his hair was long and bushy, and he had a bottle of beer stashed in his jacket. He disappeared into the school and we crouched below our homeroom windows, listening to the muffled tones of parent conversations with Miss Bailey until it seemed everyone had left. Then we heard Dad sniggering. Randy hunched over so I could stand on his back and I managed to get eye-level to the windowsill. Miss Bailey was sitting on Dad's lap, sharing his beer. She had her legs crossed and her skirt was high on her thighs.

Granddad was coming and we were all excited to see him. We'd moved into another house in Harrison that had three bedrooms and a big backyard, just a block from a real beach. He wouldn't be thrilled about the new baby but everything else would meet with his approval. The house was clean and the sheets were fresh. Mom had a stew simmering and a perfectly ripe tomato she'd picked from her potted plant.

The only problem was Dad. Mom was on the back porch trying to cut his wild hair with the buzzcutters. She kept swatting him like a disobedient dog, trying to get him to sit still.

Dad had stayed six weeks at camp and had sent his entire check home without any bar deductions so, for the moment, Mom's gratitude eclipsed her anger. She should have fed him earlier to soak up the booze, but she wanted everyone to sit together at her new green arborite kitchen table to have dinner like a family. The red chairs didn't match, that's why she got them cheap, but at least they were new. The flowers in the center were so pretty she didn't chastise me for stealing them from the neighborhood gardens.

Granddad's alpine-blue Austin Nash pulled up in front of the house. He got out and pulled his worn leather bag from the trunk. He looked much thinner and older since three years ago. When I opened the front door he barely smiled.

"Hi, Dad." Mom came forward and hugged him, a light hug, but affectionate.

"You look well dear." He patted her shoulder.

"You must be hungry after that long drive. I've got beef stew." He didn't look hungry.

"Do you want to see your room?" I was eager to show off the flowers in us girls' bedroom that would be his.

"Good heavens, is that Barbara? I didn't even recognize you, you're such a big girl."

"Such a big girl," I said, parroting his English accent. He was the only British person I'd ever met.

"But still just as silly."

"Hi, Granddad." Randy waved.

"Well, someone is going to be taller than me very soon."

"Very soon, very soon . . ." I played with the words as I pushed his bag toward his room.

"Just one moment, love."

He retrieved a fishing rod he'd left outside the door and gave it to Randy. Getting presents was unfamiliar and Randy didn't know how to respond.

"Will you take me fishing?" Granddad asked, tousling Randy's hair.

Then he pulled a wooden box from his suitcase and put it in front of me. It was his calligraphy pens, along with a new pad of paper and a worn instruction book. I was ecstatic. Mom looked troubled. I thought she might be anxious about an open bottle of ink on her new table with toddlers around, but it was something else. He'd had that box of pens her whole life.

"Hello, Harry."

Dad was in the doorway grinning. He had shaved off the sides of his scalp and shaped a thick Iroquois strip down the middle of his head.

Granddad had no reaction. "Hello, Jack," he said, with just a trace of weariness.

Here we are at Harrison Lake with Mom's one-bowl-fits-all haircut.

Granddad took us walking around the lake. We mimicked the way he swung his arms, "Hep two three four, hep two three four."

On one of those walks I saw something shiny in the sand. I always had my eyes on the ground, checking for precious stones. Granddad verified that my find was a 24-carat gold ring with a square diamond in the center. It also had little sparkly baguettes on the sides. Mom didn't own a single piece of jewelry and I was thrilled to give her such a gift, but Granddad said we had to return it to its owner. I dragged my feet while Randy and Granddad made "Ring Found" posters and tacked them on telephone poles.

Granddad let me hold the ring but what he didn't know was that I carried it in my mouth for safe-keeping. When we got home after hanging the posters, the ring was gone.

"Wake up, child," Granddad said, shaking his head.

Mom checked my poop for days. I kept hoping to see the ring on her finger. It never came out. No one came to claim

it. I still wonder if it's lodged in some organ of my body, or maybe I just dropped it that day.

Granddad was tired and there was so little time to spend with him.

"Wake up, child," I said to myself, over and over.

Granddad took us swimming. Randy and I were playing with a beach ball in the water and it started to float away. Every time I touched the ball it drifted further. We were laughing and getting manic as the ball lured us beyond the buoys. Suddenly I was struggling to breathe and couldn't get my feet behind me. Granddad swam out and ordered Randy to swim back. He put one arm around my shoulders and scooped with his other arm, in elegant strokes. His fingers curved like the scroll at the top of his letters, moving in the motion of a water mill. When we got back to shore he lay down on his back for a long time. His mouth was open and his chest moved up and down slowly. The next day he had a cold and Mom said not to bother him.

Behind the door I could hear his painful hacking. I wanted to sit with him but Mom would not let us go in. I prayed his ugly cough would go away.

Then one day I came home and the door was open. Granddad had gone to stay at Aunt Tinker's in Hollywood. As heartsick as I was, it was reassuring to know that he would be getting lots of healing sun. Mom always said everything was better in California.

Randy and I threw rocks and broke the windows of an abandoned garage and Granddad showed up in one of my dreams to give us heck. "Causing destruction is ignorant," he told us. "There's no excuse for ignorance."

I'd overheard Mom talking on the phone, saying her dad had lung cancer. Whatever that was, it sounded bad. All I could do was pray for him to get better. The Seventh Day Adventists weren't in Harrison, but there was a Pentecostal church down the street. I liked walking into a place where everyone was a stranger. I liked the quiet mood. It was very different from Sabbath school. It was a real church with adults, built-in pews, and an altar. You were supposed to be baptized before you worshipped but I couldn't get baptized without my parents there, and I didn't want to draw attention to my situation. I expected at any minute to be expelled as the daughter of heathens. Kneeling in front of an empty pew, I prayed to God, pleading for him to heal my Granddad's lungs.

When Marilyn Monroe died I wondered if Granddad knew her. We finally had a television and I watched a news special showing people gathered around her star on Hollywood Boulevard. Mom said our Aunt Tinker lived right around the corner. I was half expecting to see Granddad in the crowd. I'd never heard of Marilyn Monroe before but now her image was here. Girls at school stretched out their tops to show bare shoulders and they all whispered, "I'm Marilyn Monroe." In the end, I decided Granddad wouldn't care for someone like her.

On the first day of school after winter break, I came home and Mom was crying behind her bedroom door. Dad was standing in the hallway, as sober as he'd ever been. "Your Granddad died," he said. "Now go upstairs and think about it." That was all he said.

"It's your fault," said Randy to me, and he ran upstairs.

With my fixation on the End of Days, I never thought someone I loved would die before it was time.

I still believed the Jehovah's Witness theory that when the world ended God would arrive on a big cloud and take all the deserving people up to heaven with him. I listened for the trumpets that were supposed to summon the righteous and awaken the dead who were good, but all I heard was Mom sobbing. I wanted God to bring the cloud down now so I could go to heaven with Granddad. I prayed and prayed and searched the sky for a swelling cloud but there were no signs. I squeezed into my dark crawl space. God had ignored my prayers. That's when I lost my faith, not that God existed, but that he cared about people like me.

I go running in the perfect green field at Bobby's high school. I knead my feet into the ground and chew up the grass, trying to get some warmth through my body. I run heel-to-toe, Randy showed me that. I keep my feet on parallel tracks. I cut out that dainty-puss thing with my hands and keep my elbows in, swinging loose but tight.

Randy set a school record for the mile in grade seven. I can't remember what it was, five minutes or something. He wasn't competitive, he just ran because he liked to. I ran to defy my faulty foot, to keep up with Randy, and maybe for attention. I had a coach who noticed my strong heel-to-toe push and who thought I'd excel with special training. He started making arrangements for me to go to Vancouver to try out for some team. But any ambition of becoming a track star ended when I came home one night to find my coach and Dad high on pot, giggling as they watched *The Beverly Hillbillies* to the sound track of a Jonathan Winters comedy record. I had a broken wrist then. I was so humiliated and pissed at Dad, I locked myself in the bathroom, unraveled my cast, and shaved off my eyebrows. Dad got a big chuckle over my self-mutilation. My browless face was humiliating and my wrist didn't heal right. I never went back to track and field.

Now I run and run. My foot starts cramping. I push. One more lap. Pound and punish.

Then I limp back to my car and take out the stereo and speakers, boxes of books and dishes wrapped in towels. I leave them on the sidewalk. I imagine the Scotts watching me from their window, eating chocolate bars and commenting on the weird Williams brood.

The Hope in Leaving

After Granddad died, there were no pictures for a while, no record of our days moving from house to house in the Fraser Valley. We weren't living in the camps with Dad anymore, so that meant he was gone away working for long stretches. I didn't understand why we always had to move but I came to rely on it. If I hated where we lived or if I had a bad encounter with someone, there was always the hope in leaving and doing better the next time.

Mom found a good house in Sardis. I only saw it from the car, but it was a friendly blue with white trim. The two front windows had flower boxes filled with pansies, and the small lawn was flat and evenly green, with well-tended shrubs lining the walkway. Dad came home just in time to give the landlord a check. "A fine old veteran," Dad called him. "He served in the First and Second World War." Mom, Dad, and us kids were squeezed into Granddad's little Austin Nash, followed by a U-Haul with our belongings. We stopped at the landlord's house and Mom ran in to get the keys. The car was humming, the windows were down, and the worn leather seats smelled like Granddad.

Dad stood outside, leaning against the car, having a smoke.

Mom came walking back stricken. "Nothing good ever happens with you, Jack. Nothing." She got in the car, slammed the door, then started to rail on about how she should have listened to her Dad and gone back to Jasper. She could have worked in Banff at the hotel. Now it was too late, she was stuck "for the rest of my effing life," she said.

Dad didn't say a word. He drove past a motel on the road and pulled over. A hasty conference was held outside the car, then Mom pulled us out and Dad drove off with the U-Haul.

Mom herded us over to the motel's entrance and told me and Randy to keep out of sight.

"But what about our new house?" I whined.

"We're not living there."

"But why?"

"Shush! Just keep an eye on where I go. Make sure no one sees you."

I hated being around Mom when she was agitated like this, even though I knew, whatever the problem was, it was Dad's fault.

Randy and I stood behind a dust-covered bush and started pitching rocks at a garbage can across the road. The rocks got bigger and swifter until someone shouted:

"What the hell are you doing!"

An old lady was yelling from the motel parking lot. Mom and the girls were behind her.

"Get out of here, you stupid kids!" she shrieked some more.

We ran out of sight, scared that we'd blown Mom's cover.

We figured we were hiding because the motel wouldn't rent her a room with so many kids. We peered through the bushes and watched as Mom went to the last door on the strip. She looked around and left the door open. We sat watching the office until the sun went down, then we slithered across the lot like stealth commandos.

We all found places to curl up around the room. In the dark, I heard Randy whispering to Mom, "What did Dad do?"

"It's not his fault." Her mood had softened. "They're just not very nice people."

"But why don't they want us living there?"

"Go to sleep."

"Why, Mom?"

She didn't say anything for a while. Then she spoke like she needed to say it to believe it.

"They said they don't believe in mixed marriages."

That kept me thinking for hours. It was never really acknowledged that Dad was Indian. He was just kind of dark. Real Indians lived on reservations.

I'd barely closed my eyes, then Mom was hushing us out into the darkness. She carried Marlene, and Randy carried Kate as we scurried out of the parking lot to the spot where Dad had left us on the road. He was waiting with the U-Haul.

We squeezed into Granddad's car and slept until we reached our new home, a crappy little shack with all the kids piled in one room. The yard was a mess of dandelions that sprouted up past the windowsills.

At our new school there was a boy named David that the kids called Stinky. His cheeks were always red and his lower lip stuck out. He had a thick body and wore overalls. I felt sorry for him so I talked to him, though he was slow to reply.

I was having lunch on the playground while Randy shot hoops by himself. David sat a few feet away, silently eating stew from a mason jar. He had stubby hands that were covered with rings of weeping blisters popping out of scaly skin. Randy and I guessed he had a bad case of ringworm. Mom was always telling us not to pet animals because they might have ringworm and it was very contagious. David's family were farmers, so I figured he must have caught it from a cow.

Kids started teasing, "Stinky's got a girlfriend!"

"His name's David," I said, defending him, though I wished the girls would invite me to play tetherball.

One afternoon, I was coming from the washroom. David had a detention and was standing in the cloakroom. As I passed, he grabbed me from behind and tried to hug me. His fleshy hands were hot and moist. The sweat and pus and dead skin rubbed under my bare arms. I shook him loose and ran to class. At home I scrubbed my arms and doused them with detanol. I checked constantly to see if sores had erupted, but thankfully they never came. After that, I stayed away from David.

Randy was finally joined by some boys on the basketball court. The ball hit him in the head, his eyes teared up, but he kept playing. Then the ball hit him again and again. The boys kept pretending it was accidental. Randy chose not to fight back. He walked off the court and after that spent lunches with me until, soon enough, we moved.

We had a pit stop in Chilliwack on a poor man's picket fence kind of street. The lawn was decent and the house was freshly painted white, but it was really just a cabin with two very small bedrooms. A teenage boy named Lorne lived next door. He had handsome whiteish blue eyes like a husky and black lashes. I pretended I could tap dance and put on a show for him. He was amused by me, and I liked talking to him. He had rabbits in a pen and used to let me hold them. Once a bunny was mounted on another bunny, and Lorne said, "That's what I'm going to do to you." That put a stop to my tap dances.

Rosedale

Then we moved to Rosedale, to the gravel pit house. That's when the curse kicked in.

When we drove through the town there were people standing by the road, holding up signs. They were Doukhobors who had come to Canada to escape religious persecution in Russia. They lived in communes and burned their possessions to denounce materialism. Dad was as antimaterialist as they come, but he couldn't resist making fun of them. From the local newspaper, he tore out a blurry picture of a group of Doukhobors circled naked around a bonfire of their clothes. He wrote on it, "Would you like to go to their next weenie roast, Simone?" and taped it to the wall.

Mom and Dad were having more laughs than usual. Fire season had come early in the bush and the logging camps were shut down, so Dad had been around to help us get settled. He was still in work mode, getting up early and staying sober while he looked for a summer job.

We'd moved into a big old ramshackle farmhouse beside a

gravel pit. It had four bedrooms and a greenhouse for a front porch. There were all kinds of fruit trees, a big grassy yard, and old barns filled with rusty machinery from when it was a working farm. There was endless exploring to be done.

A boy named Garry came riding his bike down our long driveway one day. I was instantly smitten. He was blond, tall, and absolutely normal. He and Randy became friends. We ran across the barn roof like guerrilla soldiers, jumping down and rolling in the tall grass. Once the boys put a garter snake in my gumboot and it bit my toe. I was horrified, but I picked it up by the tail and chased them with it. I was tolerated if I could play like a boy.

For a moment in June, wild strawberries turned ripe on a hillside and we scrambled up the slope, our bodies pressed into the warm earth, shoving every little red gem into our mouths until the hill was stripped bare. We ran in bliss through the clouds of pesticide sprayed by the crop dusters on the neighboring cornfields.

At night I hugged my pillow, pretending it was Garry. But when we went to Garry's place, a feeling of not being good enough washed over me. His home was the neatest, most perfect place I'd seen. The furniture seemed like it came from another century but still looked new. His mother brought us milk and cookies on a tray. She wore a checkered apron and her hair was smooth and wavy, like she'd just come from a beauty parlor. She asked all kinds of questions about us, like where we came from and what Dad did for a living. Dad had just gone off to sell peavey sticks in Vancouver and for some reason I thought that sounded more respectable than being a logger. I explained that peavey sticks were used to spear logs and pull them into booms. She shook her head saying, "Isn't that interesting?" and that she'd like to meet my mom. I nodded sure, but I knew it would never happen. Mom was too shy to meet people.

Garry's house was on the other side of a slough that we crossed on a one-lane bridge. They had a huge maple tree with a giant tire on a rope that swung over the edge of the slough. We played like little monkeys until Garry's dad drove up and told us it was time to go. He had on a suit and carried a small suitcase. I thought he might be coming from a funeral but Garry said he wore suits everyday because he was a lawyer in Chilliwack. I was glad Dad wasn't around for Garry to see how he dressed. That night I squeezed my pillow and cried because I knew Garry would never love someone like me.

Our trio expanded when Cheryl and her little brother came across the highway and offered to cut our grass for fifty cents. We didn't have fifty cents, but they let us use their lawn mower and we cut it ourselves. They were real farmers. We helped them round up their geese with big sticks and forced them into their shed. In the rain, the geese would be slipping and sliding on the poop-covered ramp, spitting and trying to bite us. After dinner we'd sneak down to the bull field. Randy would get twenty feet from the herd. We'd be following him about forty feet back. He'd stand still, locking eyes with the biggest bull, then he'd yell "Come on!" and we'd run like hell as it chased us. We'd hurl ourselves over the fence and the bull would come to a dead halt, seething on the other side of the barbed wire. That's why Garry liked Randy, I could tell. Randy was fearless.

On hot days, we all walked a mile down the trail behind our house to a backwater of the Frazer River and swam in the muddy water. We ate wild huckleberries on the trail, then the salmonberries got ripe, then the thimbleberries, and in late summer we filled up on endless blackberries. Mom got a job so Randy and I had to pull Kate and Marlene in a wagon along with us. Splashing and spinning on an inner-tube was the best way to babysit a three-year-old.

One hot day, Garry's mom drove the long way around to meet us at the backwater. She wore sandals with plastic flowers on top, a one-piece flower bathing suit with a little see-through sun jacket, and a straw hat. She was perfection stretched out a striped beach blanket.

"Where's your mother?" she called out.

"At work," I yelled back.

She came down to the water's edge. "What is she thinking, leaving ten-year-olds with a baby?" I was nine but didn't correct her.

Her eyes were like dark blue jewels, but the rouge on her cheeks looked odd in this light. Her nose was quite pointed and without lipstick her mouth almost disappeared.

"When is she coming home?"

Her voice made my heart pound. Garry was looking at me with the same blue eyes as his mother. I wondered if he'd said bad things about us. His nose was peeling and his shoulders were bright red against skinny white arms. For the first time, I noticed that his chest sort of caved in and made him look weak.

"I'm going to take the baby home with me and your mother can pick her up when she gets back."

She tried to lift Kate out of the inner tube, but Kate kicked up a fury, soaking Garry's mother's outfit and pummeling her in the stomach. Kate was a hefty girl and when she lashed out she could do damage. She screamed like she was being hurt and Garry's mother backed off.

"I'll take her home now," I said. "My mom will be back soon."

I carried Kate to the wagon. Randy and Marlene fell in behind me.

Garry stood by his mother's side. That night my pillow would be just a pillow.

The bonfires came, burning brush and leaves, the smell of summer dying into fall. Cheryl's cousin Chuck came from Chilliwack to help bale hay. He and Randy threw bales on the flatbed and we stacked them. Then we drove down the highway on top of the bales and Chuck intoxicated us with scary stories. "I'm on the first step, Johnny. I'm at your door now, Johnny. I'm in your bedroom, Johnny . . . Gotcha!" and we squealed. We felt so naughty huddled together as the night grew dark and the air grew colder. At their Grandma Ludivik's place we drank her special tea, a sweet milky brew. Her house smelled like old meat and cat urine, but the tea was delicious and Chuck kept us laughing. We were just settling into fifth grade at another school, and I was already wishing we were leaving. Garry was in sixth grade, so it was easy for him to avoid us. When I did catch sight of him, my heart would kind of knock against my ribs because he looked so handsome in his new school clothes. I didn't love him, I think I just wanted a life like his.

Randy was more affected by Garry's rejection. It would have made things better if he'd had a friend at school. He started getting into little scuffles, in the hall, in the boys' bathroom. Some kids called us Doukhobors and Randy picked up a desk and threw it at them. He got the strap a few times and was always getting detentions. When the final bell rang, Randy would fly out of school. I'd sprint after him but I could never keep up. He was most comfortable in his body when he was running. He had Mom's long legs and Dad's agility bounding down the road with light strides, more energized as he ran. He'd run the entire two miles home then double back and lope along with me.

Dad came back home with a bunch of unsold peavey sticks. Randy and I really wanted to take one but Mom didn't want us running around with a five-foot-long steel-headed spear. Dad tried to sell them out of the trunk of his car when he'd go to the local legion hall, but there wasn't a big demand for peaveys in a farming community. Mom and Dad had been getting along, but over the days, as his peaveys went unsold and his drinking increased, so did their fights, until all we heard at night was Mom bombarding Dad with fury and tears.

"Everything's falling down in this house, there's rats everywhere!"

"Just get a cat," he told her.

"I don't want a bloody cat. You buy the whole goddamn lower mainland a drink and leave us with nothing."

She'd do a really nasty imitation of him. "Have another beer on me, I don't need to pay my oil bill, forget about the rent. Who cares if my kids don't get fed?"

Dad would murmur something like, "Now, now, there's always grub on the table."

Mom would throw a dish at him and the sound of it shattering would feel like our family breaking apart. Lying in bed, I would sing "Ring Around the Rosy" to myself, and I'd imagine all of us holding hands and skipping in a circle, louder and faster until the sound of the fighting was obliterated.

On Sundays, Cheryl and I danced in secret ecstasy to The Beatles while Grandma Ludivik beheaded chickens. We watched ourselves in the mirror of her old country trousseau, our rapture intensified by the sacrifice of animals outside the window. I'd given up the hymns of Sunday mass. I'd stopped praying for Mom to smile or for Dad to come back. I just wanted to be seventeen, to skip the seven-year sentence in between and be out on a city street to catch the eye of some hipster from another continent. *Make his heart go boom, as I crossed the room, and he'd hold his hand in miiieeeene . . .*

Grandma Ludivik walked in on us, smearing bloody hands on her ancient apron, and I ran out, slamming the screen door behind me like a heathen.

Her squawks of disapproval carried over the fields as I skipped home.

I drive to Denny's to meet Misty and Marlene.

They've been talking for a while. Marlene must be telling Misty what she knows. Misty wasn't close to Randy. Marlene has a troubled history with her, and I don't know why she wants to be part of this family. It didn't work out, she should be thankful.

I place an order at the counter and down a glass of milk

to stop my legs from cramping. I still have time to catch the last ferry.

Misty puts on a sympathetic face.

I've had the same reaction to her face since the first time she came to our door looking for Dad. I think she was fifteen, though I can't be sure. She had bleach-orange hair with black roots and a face just like Dad's. It was a pretty face, but she had a dirty laugh and an exaggerated wiggle when she walked that bugged me. She said her name was Terry. She'd escaped from a detention home and tracked Dad down through the Seamen's Union. She had a younger sister, Dana, who later called herself Helen.

Mom says their mother was a prostitute, but that could just be Mom's opinion. Their mother met Dad—aka Jack, RJ, Handsome Jack, or John—during his short stint as a welterweight boxer in Vancouver. I've never been able to get the facts straight on how the kids came to live with Dad's parents. One story was that Dad was overseas, stationed in Norway during the Korean War when his wife ran off, but the dates don't add up. Whatever the circumstances, Misty and Dana were raised by Dad's parents, eventually coming to settle in the house that Mom lives in now. The house with the note on the door.

I never thought about whether Dad had a mother and father until Misty showed up. Dad just seemed to come out of the dirt. His parents had long ago washed their hands of him, but with the coming of Misty a dispirited reunion came to pass. Their house was my idea of normal, especially the fake wood dining table with matching chairs and a chandelier hanging above. The rooms were neat and deliberate, but they also seemed to lack oxygen. All of us kids grew very sleepy.

Helen was a withered smoker with skinny blue legs and freshly rolled grey hair. Walton was the Indian, quiet and handsomely sad, dressed in proper worn clothes. He was a proofreader for the *Victoria Times*. That sounded very important to me. He was once the editor of a big newspaper in Edmonton but lost his job and all his money because he was a bad drinker. Now he was white-knuckle sober. My brothers and sisters and I were like stray mutts with muddy feet. Walton and Helen had little to say to us. They watched hockey on TV in odd reverence, jerking involuntarily at goals and skirmishes. Sometimes I noticed Helen looking at Dad with a puzzled expression. Randy and I ate a million walnuts and I got a canker.

All together we went to the high school gymnasium to hear an orchestra that Dana was playing the flute in. I kept trying to peek at her through the reeds but couldn't get a good visual, then we left before it was over, so I didn't meet her. That's all I remember of our visit with Dad's parents. I guess Misty decided she wanted to stay with us. It made no sense to me why she would choose a rat-infested, drafty old shack over a house with a chandelier and matching furniture.

Marlene's grief is dry, her tears have imploded. Marijuana is not suited for sad occasions. There's nothing to giggle about. Not that I giggled on marijuana, I went mute. I can't go near the stuff.

"How are you feeling, Barb?"

"I'm tired."

"Randy was suffering for a long time."

I don't want to share my sadness with her.

My meatless chef salad arrives, but it's not meatless enough. I edge it away. One of Marlene's eyes is bugging out while the other is narrowed, staring at the salad as if the garbanzo beans are speaking to her.

Misty picks at a tomato slice from my salad while she talks about the impermanence of life. "Death is just the end of the body, the spirit lives on."

She's a Buddhist now. Her hands turn in as if she's concealing something. She's smart and she talks in an elevated way, but I don't trust her hands.

One time Mom found a bundle of letters addressed to Dad from Dana, Misty's younger sister, the flute player. They were a series of pleas: "Please could I come visit," "Please write me back," "Please let me be a part of your family," "Please tell me what I've done wrong," "Please tell me why you hate me." Mom couldn't be sure who hid them in the drawer but she suspected Misty. Mom had never seen them and was certain Dad hadn't either. It is doubtful Dad would have even responded adequately, but that doesn't lessen the crime.

"Where are you going to stay?" Misty asks.

The air conditioning has made me cold again. Now Misty's hand curls around a package of Export A's. I'm dying for a smoke but not from her.

"I'm not sure."

I haven't thought about where I'll stay. I'll just stay awake.

I'm not in a class to consider a hotel. I'm still hoping to get to Toronto. My ex-boyfriend loaned me a thousand dollars. My airline ticket took up a chunk of that. I'll stay at the Y until I find an apartment. I'll have to pay first and last month's rent, plus the deposit. I'll make two hundred and fifty dollars a week for the play, if I can get there.

Marlene mentions that Kate is staying at her place to eliminate an option that would be uncomfortable for both of us.

"How's Kate?" Misty tries another entry under our family skin.

"She just got back from Europe," Marlene says. "She doesn't know yet."

"Who's staying at Ryan Street?"

"Mom and Bobby, I guess. The guys cleaned up Randy's room."

I don't want to hear this. What they cleaned up, who cleaned up, how many people were there.

Randy's body floats through my thoughts. Where is his body? What has it been doing these last few hours? He died when the sun came out. There was nothing more he could do. There was blood, I'm sure. Maybe I'm wrong. Maybe we're all wrong. Maybe he's lying on a metal gurney in a locked room, shivering. I should find out where he is, but if he wants to live, he'll live. If he wants to die, there's nothing I can do.

I go outside and call my ex-boyfriend collect on a payphone. "Hey."

"Are you at the airport? Got your list?" Ty asks with his ever-chipper tone of encouragement.

He's given me a list of agents, writers, and actors to contact in Toronto. He's been working on me to take a more professional approach to my career. Even though I broke it off with him, he's still helping me.

"Ya ... No ... I ..." I can't bring myself to say the words. He asks if I'm all right and I start to whimper, "It's my brother."

He vaguely guesses what's happened.

"Do you want me to come over?"

On the one hand I do, but it would be too awkward. It's not the best time to meet my family.

"I'm all right. I just wanted you to know."

"I'll come over," he insists. But I can't help thinking he sees this as an opportunity to get close to me again.

"No. Please don't. Thanks again for the list."

I hang up before he can convince me otherwise.

"Barb," Marlene's voice bursts through my thoughts, "me and Misty need a ride." I drop Misty at some hippie house. Marlene looks like she's on the verge of crying, but can't connect with her tears, like when you're trying to sneeze but don't. We drive together in silence.

Red

Dad is on the phone. "Yep, yep, yep, mmm, yep, yep. Alright then, we'll see you in the AM."

"Red is on his way," he announces.

Red is Dad's oldest and best friend. Everybody likes Red, even Mom. He's a world traveler with great stories, but he's also one of us. He grew up with Dad in Alberta.

"All the way from Brixton. He's going standby."

It's not surprising. Red is a selfless person, kind of saintly. He's Dad's opposite in every way: fair-skinned, red-haired, ascetic, self-disciplined. Unlike many of Dad's friends, Red looks out for Dad. They share a fascination with the rougher side of life. They appreciate solitude and work until their bodies break, but Red doesn't need to reward himself with alcohol. It's good news he's coming.

Red and Dad hopped a freight train heading west from Lamont when they were fifteen. Dad was running away from the fallout of a romantic entanglement with an older woman. His mother blew the whistle after intercepting a revealing love letter, and the woman was brought up on charges, though Red tells me Dad was the least innocent of the two. The woman was the wife of a soldier and Dad was apparently tutoring her in math. The romantic entanglement is not a stretch, but the tutoring is surprising. Dad has never taught me anything more than how to whittle and tie knots. Red insists that Dad was a brilliant student and made extra money tutoring. Dad's mother used to tell people that he fell off a truck and hit his head to explain his behavior.

Red was escaping the suffocation of an overprotective family. He says his mother gave him antibiotics so frequently she wiped out his immune system, so he made it a lifelong goal to build his strength. Dad was all dirt and thick-skinned resistance. They balanced each other out. Together they worked on the Pacific railroad, in the copper mines, and finally in the logging camps of British Columbia. Dad was the motor and Red kept them on an even keel. It's as though Red took vicarious protection from the elements under Dad's thick skin, and Dad's drinking seemed more reasonable in Red's presence.

During fire season, Red would periodically sleep on our couch. It was fun having him around because he was always mobilizing the family to go on outings. Once he got Dad to compete in a logrolling contest at Green Point. Green Point was at the end of a narrow winding mountain highway with sheer cliffs that dropped into a glacial lake. The drive terrified me. I sat in the front on Red's knee, looking out at the twisting horizon, trying not to get sick.

Dad didn't want his name on record because he was still

collecting worker's compensation for some broken fingers, so he entered as Handsome Jack. When they called "Handsome Jack" over the loudspeakers there were chuckles amongst the loggers.

Dad and another logger stood side-by-side, facing in opposite directions on a log about sixteen inches around. They steadied themselves until the announcer fired the starting gun and we saw the most frenetic foot action. Whoever got the advantage ran forward at a whirlwind pace, while the other man had to run backward. The log spun, came to a stop, lurched and then reversed as Dad and his opponent tried to shake each other off. Dad won second prize, I think it was twenty dollars. Red didn't compete because he was a high rigger not a boom man, but Dad still pushed him into the lake.

In a car packed with four kids, two soaking-wet men, and Mom, Dad pulled over on the way home to pick up an Indian couple who were hitchhiking. Mom said, "Don't you dare." But Dad told her, "They'll be walking all night. How would you feel if they got run over?"

It had happened a few times that I could remember, Native people hit by cars on the road at night.

Red and Mom sat in back with us kids piled up on them, and the couple squeezed into the front seat beside Dad. There wasn't enough air to talk and then the woman passed a garlic salami in front of my face. Mom and I were gagging but Dad took a big bite.

The woman was studying Dad's profile and said, "I don't know how handsome you are Jack, but you sure are conceited."

In the morning, Randy and I found the couple nestled on

our back porch under Dad's work clothes, a caulk boot under each of their heads. We managed to step over them without waking them up on our way to school.

"Kate's on her way," Marlene says as she cleans up after Dad.

For someone with so few belongings, Dad manages to leave a hefty trail of detritus. He's got a musty old sleeping bag stretched out on the balcony. Hanging over the rail are rinsed out socks and a T-shirt. The latest issue of the *New Yorker* lies face-down on the couch, with a library copy of *Another Roadside Attraction* beside it, and an ashtray is overflowing with old butts and whittled wood. Maybe he's sharpening sticks to roast hot dogs on the balcony, I wonder.

Mom and Marlene have become neat freaks. Our homes were never neat after Mom racked up five kids and started working full-time, but now she's obsessed, as if she's trying to clean up the past.

Max's claws grip Marlene's shoulder while she vacuums up ashes. His little blue head bobs up and down like he's on a boat in rough water. I don't get her bird love. I don't like beaks anywhere close to my eyes. She sticks out her lower lip for Max to nibble.

I take a shower but I can't get the water warm enough. I change into the only clothes I packed in my backpack, a white T-shirt and a thrift store floral skirt. Mom hates old things. She couldn't stand it when I used to hitchhike up the peninsula on Saturdays to buy clothes at the Women's Hospital Auxiliary. She had no praise when I'd make a funky shift from a fat lady's dress on the sewing machine that once belonged to her mother. I could transform a fifty-cent cast-off into something special. I couldn't afford new clothes so I did my own thing.

"Those are dead people's clothes," Mom would say.

Now for the first time, I am repelled by the leftover scent of someone else on the skirt, but it's all I have with me. From Marlene's spartan medicine chest I take a dab of blush and a smooch of eyeliner, but the makeup looks sad sitting on my face so I rub it off.

My youngest sister Kate is bent over on the couch with her hands to her face. Marlene stares blankly while Max chews on her earlobe. Dad stands grimacing. Mom hovers over Kate with a hand stiffly reaching out, barely touching her head.

I've learned in improvisation classes that it's best to jump into the heart of awkwardness, rather than to go cold on the fringes.

"Hi, Kate." I sit, putting a sisterly arm around her. She's become a giant. Just three years ago she was little, now at eighteen she is the tallest girl of the bunch. I feel how muscular she is and remember that she's living with a kayak builder up-island, paddling in the sea.

The news has broadsided her. She came down for a little visit, to show pictures from her trip to Europe.

Her face glistens with tears. She has an appealing face, healthy and intelligent. I pat her arm but I'm not convincing in the role of comforter.

"Would you like some tea, Kate?" Mom asks.

Kate shakes her head. "Where's Bobby?"

Bobby and Kate are closest in age and sensibility. Since I've left home, they've become allies.

"At Paul's."

A few more sobs spill out. She scans our faces, searching for some trace of solidarity. She must have learned solidarity exists while traveling with her mates, hitchhiking, sleeping in hostels and on the floors of farmhouses—that one-for-all-andall-for-one sense that propels you to keep your head above water. These heads are sinking.

"Do you want a valium?" Dad asks.

Kate looks at him with no response. Her eyes are greener than I remember. She is soft and sensitive, but rational, not so vulnerable to the family vortex. She stands. She must be almost six feet tall.

"I'm going to go see Bobby," she says and makes her exit.

The walls are closing in on me.

"I just have to get something at the store," I say and grab my purse.

"Can you get some half-and-half?" Marlene asks.

"Sure."

"I'll go with you," Mom offers.

"No, no. I'll be quick." I leave without looking at her.

I sprint to my car and peel off to catch that last ferry. I roll down the windows to fill my lungs with island air. Mom doesn't need me. Maybe she'd even prefer me not to be here.

What should I do with the car? I was leaving it for Randy but the gesture didn't fool him. He knew it was skin I was shedding in my move to finally ditch him. And everyone else.

In the gravel pit house, I stepped on a near-dead rat with desiccated eyes and its poisoned guts squished up between my toes. I begged Mom to get a cat to kill the rats, but she'd become superstitious about cats and witches. They burned the cats of Europe for the same reason, then rats ran free to spread the plague. But she didn't think about things like that.

Mom and Dad were fighting. I was in bed singing "Ring Around the Rosy" to myself. It was bad. Even Dad yelled before he slammed the door and disappeared into the night.

Under the searchlight of a full moon bearing down on our living room, a rat sniffed Randy's face while he slept. Mom was hiding out in the bathroom.

"You love your dad, don't you?" Her voice was like a spider bite.

I pushed the door open. She was sitting on the toilet seat, her nose shiny, mascara smudged under her eyes. A half-hearted trickle of blood from a cut wrist cried out on her white waitress uniform where another baby was bursting through the buttons.

"I love you too," I wanted to say, but I knew it wouldn't sound right.

"Your dad will look after you."

Saying Dad would look after us was like saying we were done for.

The smudges under her eyes spread down her face while I put gauze on her wrist.

Randy fetched the change he had pilfered from Dad's pockets and pooled it with Mom's tips. I got her tatty old coat to cover up the bloodstains on her uniform, and we drove ten miles to the A&W drive-in. We had root beer floats and french fries. Mom didn't die and we all went home to bed.

The terminal is up ahead. Cars disembark, I think I can make it. I can't think beyond the boat, what I'll do with the car at the airport, or where I'll stay. About the play. I can't think about that. I just have to get on board. I can't think about money. I can't think about family. I just have to go. I can't help anyone.

Cars slowly roll onto the ferry. I'm approaching the ticket booth. I pull out some cash.

One day I'll come back and we'll all mourn. We'll lay a wreath, hold hands, and sing "Ring Around the Rosy."

The window is closed. The guy is there, talking over the loudspeaker, but the fucking window is closed. I feel a rush of anger. I want to get out and pound the window. Put my fists through the glass. Like I did when I was five years old and the front door was locked. Glass is everywhere, so normal, transparent, a constant threat. My grandmother broke a wine glass against the table one night during dinner and cut her wrist, just like that. Randy cut his neck with a glass ashtray he broke in a psychologist's office. The doctor turned on Mom. He said, "What have you done to this beautiful boy?"

The voices came through breaking glass. In the gravel pit house. Late at night. I was startled awake by a loud crash. Before I could guess what I'd heard, there was another crash. It was outside the house. *Crash smash crash*. I couldn't understand where it was coming from. The next shattering sounded like a window in the house. More shattering, smashing, cracking, then a tinkle of shards like an evil laugh.

Mom was downstairs in her room. I heard whispering. They were inside the house, creeping around. I wondered if they were people Dad knew? Someone he owed money to, or someone he pissed off with one of his jokes? We had nothing to rob. *Crack, smash,* more glass was broken than there were windows in our house. I imagined dark figures smashing bottles against the wall and kicking the pieces across the floor. Then the dark figures were in Mom's room. I was petrified. I imagined them cutting her. I wanted to call her but I couldn't find my voice. I lowered my feet to the floor.

I stepped, then listened for a muffled cry, or the shuffle of struggling bodies. Between the breakings, malevolent voices, barely audible but intensely present, whispered their mischief. I had to get to Mom. I moved one step, paused, then another, down the L-shaped stairs, step, pause, step. When I got to the corner, I screamed out, "Mom!" There was silence, then "Barbara!" She sounded okay. I ran to the bottom of the stairs and met her there. She put her hands on my shoulders and we stood together shaking. She'd heard what I heard, the glass breaking and the voices. We turned on the living room light. The front window was intact. We walked through the entire house. There were no signs of broken glass.

All the other kids slept through it.

In the morning, we walked around the house and into the gravel pit but there was no glass anywhere. We sometimes talk about it, wondering if maybe the gravel pit was dug over a burial ground and the spirits woke up. Or maybe it was a milk truck on the road being ransacked by drunken teenagers.

"Just one adult?" the guy in the ticket booth asks me. I feel like a criminal unable to carry out my crime.

I can't leave Mom now. There's too much glass everywhere.

"I'm sorry," I say. "I made a mistake." I do a U-turn and head back to Victoria.

Back at Marlene's, I pick up Mom and drive to the Ryan Street house. We say nothing about the stack of boxes I've left on the sidewalk. When we reach the door, Mom ignores the note.

Inside it is weirdly hot and there's a strong smell of hospital disinfectant. Mom sets about opening the windows and doors.

My head is light and my knees wobble. I look in the kitchen for saltines. Mom always has saltines, her cure-all for queasiness. The kitchen is stifling. The oven has been on all day. On the counter is a sheet of baked cookies and a bowl of batter. I am instantly cold when Mom opens the back door.

"Do you want some warm milk?"

The thought of warm milk makes me gag, but it'll help me sleep.

Mom busies herself at the counter, taking the batter into the bathroom and flushing it away. She hesitates with the baked cookies. They're chocolate chip, perfectly browned and evenly shaped.

"He came into the kitchen and said it made him happy to see me baking cookies."

She stares at the little treats that have betrayed her.

"He seemed better this last week. He was looking forward to having your car, said he was going to go pick peaches in the Okanagan."

For the first time, it occurs to me that Randy couldn't have had a driver's license. I was rushing to give him my car without knowing if he'd ever driven.

The milk boils over, creating a stink on the element. Mom

pours what's left into cups. She gets a pillow, a clean sheet, and a Hudson Bay blanket and puts them on the couch. The blanket is older than I am. It's surprising she's kept it around. Mom stores clothes and linens with bars of soap to keep them fresh. She learned that from her mother, and I learned it from her.

The living room is furnished with pieces I made in woodworking—a black-walnut french-pavilion end table, a matching coffee table, and a little chess table I made from a maple burl. I inlayed yellow cedar and black walnut squares to make the board, then made the men out of white clay and red clay. There's a lamp I spun on the lathe and wired up myself. All skills usurped from Randy.

Mom brings out a big green suitcase.

"I bought this for Randy's trip to the Okanagan. I thought you could take it."

It still has the price tag on. The rare times that Mom buys something, she always holds onto the option of returning it.

"You sure you don't want to return it?"

"No, you should take it."

It's a big suitcase and I only have a few pieces of clothing, but I want Mom to feel like she's given me something important, so I take it.

As she retreats to her bedroom with the cup of milk, she turns at the door and tries to say something but gives up.

Light seeps from under the door, her secret grief escaping.

I am on the plane to Toronto. Randy is sitting beside me, his stiff posture more exaggerated than usual. His back is board-straight and he's looking forward. His body moves as if connected by metal rods. His head turns, then his torso. He doesn't bend but swivels. He doesn't seem to be aware of me. His mouth's a Kabuki frown and his eyes are fixed in space. I look down and see he's bleeding from his stomach. Hemorrhaging. Blood is gushing out of him, running down his clothes and onto my white running shoes. People are leaving the plane, so there is no one to help me. I take off my white T-shirt and press it into the wound, and it's instantly saturated. Randy continues to ignore me. I sneak away, shirtless. The theater director is standing at the open door. He tells me I have to be on stage now. There's a shortcut through the airport bathroom, which brings me backstage. From the wings I can see the audience is waiting. The director points for me to go on. I step out. I'm wearing the shitty floral skirt, my shoes have blood on them, I'm bare-breasted. I can't remember my first line. I can't remember the name of the play.

Dad and Red jolt me awake as they barge through the front door. I wrap the bedsheet around me and exit to the bathroom. There's not much I can do to refresh myself. I start to fold up the sheet when I see a big red blotch on it. I wish I could lie down in the bathtub and disappear, but I scrub out the bloody sheet and hang it up. I perform the necessary ablutions and put the anonymous dead person's skirt back on.

Dad is checking out the new suitcase, unzipping the different compartments, admiring its sturdiness.

"It's for Barbara." Mom stops him before he gets any ideas.

"Lucky you." Dad pushes it aside.

"Well you certainly have filled out," Red says. The comment is meant to be approving, but it makes me self-conscious of my breasts.

"You were just a slip of a thing last time I saw you."

Red looks like a Viking. He's thin and soft-spoken, but he's capable of hacking someone's head off. He has fierce eyes and bushy red brows. He's one of my favorite people, though mostly I know him through the letters he writes Dad. Since leaving Canada, he has hitchhiked across India, been a lifeguard in Australia, and now he's a mailman in South London.

"Jack tells me you've become a good runner," Red says.

"I bet you can't keep up with Red," Dad challenges.

I feel rotten but I won't make excuses. This is typical of Dad. He squashed my interest in becoming a competitive runner when he corrupted my coach, and now he wants me to run. He used to tell me I sounded like I was in pain when I sang and that I should learn classical music—as if I could by myself—but if he had friends over, he'd put me on the spot by insisting I sing a song for them.

"Wanna do laps at the high school or run the bluffs at Beacon Hill park?" I step up.

"This is mile zero of the eight-thousand kilometer Trans-Canada Highway."

Red gives me a lesson on the history of Beacon Hill while we jog under weeping willows, past the multicolored rose garden, toward a grove of ancient Douglas firs.

"It got its name from two beacons that used to be on the hill. The westernmost was a blue triangle and the other a green square. If a sailor could see the square through the triangle it meant he was on Brotchie Ledge, which meant he was in trouble."

After my body's sluggishness burns off, we sprint full-out

on the ocean walkway. I'm energized by the salt air. Not talking, not thinking, just galloping along.

The heaviness returns as we walk back through the park.

"Your dad never got a degree in child-rearing. He was capable of an academic career, he was that smart. But he was an adventurer, he was drawn to the outdoors. He's very accomplished in his work. You know, he paid a big price, broke his back, wrecked his knees, lost his teeth. He's like a soldier, prouder of his wounds than his wages, which was unfortunate for his family, I guess. He just thought that what worked for him would work for Randy but, you know, times have changed. Randy was a more sensitive kind of person. He always worried me. You were special, Randy was trickier."

"Randy was more special than me. He had all the gifts."

I use the past tense, not because I'm thinking of Randy as dead, but because in the last ten years, he'd lost his gifts. It's like they transferred to me while he was ill.

I never accepted the idea that Randy's mental illness was a permanent condition. It was a shared temporary malady, like when we had the measles, mumps, or chicken pox. If one of us got sick, it was impossible not to infect the other, and usually one of us got hit harder. When Randy had a mild case of whooping cough, I was wiped out for months. I got over the voices in my head, but he never did.

Red rips the note down.

"'Go to the Scott's house next door.' Hmmm. I guess this is no longer relevant." He says, crumpling it up.

Dad is ironing a shirt. He's clear-headed. Mom is preparing tea.

"Simone and I have to go down to the . . ." Dad mumbles.

I hear "beer parlor" and have a flash of anger, then I realize he said "funeral parlor."

"Kate's meeting us there."

Mom sets the tea down with the chocolate chip cookies she baked for Randy the day before. She hates to waste. She won't eat one, she knows I won't, but Red and Dad are clueless.

Red goes off to see his "old Aunt Mary" with the cookies. Dad has an old Aunt Mary too. They must be the same person, they live in the same area. It's not unusual that I don't know a relative, but I'm confused over whose aunt she really is.

"Did you find a picture?" Mom asks. "I thought maybe you could make a little thing for the service."

I didn't realize that's why she gave me the chocolate box. It seems premature to talk about the service before we've talked about the death. For a moment, Mom's eyes connect with mine and my entire body shudders. It's too overwhelming to discuss. How terrible it is to be a mother.

It must have been a school night, because we were in bed early. I heard a cry of distress.

"Get my purse!" Mom yelled. She was in labor.

She wedged herself behind the steering wheel and we lurched our way to the hospital in Chilliwack. Every time she had a contraction Mom would slow the car down and moan like an animal in a leg trap. Then she would double her speed until the next contraction.

She parked as close as she could to the entrance and told us to keep the car doors locked. Then she lumbered up to the admitting area holding her purse, and some nurses ran up with a wheelchair.

We waited in the cold car. Randy was in the front seat staring at the hospital entrance, expecting Mom to come back any moment. Us girls were in the backseat, tugging on Mom's coat that she'd left behind for warmth. Kate was in the middle, whining in frustrated sleepiness. I started making *brrr* noises with my lips to distract her. Marlene joined in and then it became a game with Kate making loud raspberries. Eventually her *brrrs* became murmurs and then little snores.

It was late January and the car got colder as the hours passed. I didn't think this night would ever end, but suddenly it was daybreak and we were being awakened by a man in uniform tapping on the window.

Randy took charge, rolling down the window.

"Where are your parents?" the man asked, staring at each one of us.

"Inside. Our mom's having a baby. Our dad went in a minute ago."

The guy walked away but kept looking back.

We all had to go to the bathroom, so we shuffled into the hospital after him.

A woman at the reception desk pointed us in the direction of the washrooms, and when we returned she called a nurse who took us up to see Mom.

The room was warm. A swaddled bundle was resting on Mom's chest. Mom's face was all new, she had no trouble in her eyes, and her smile was big and peaceful. Kate threw herself on the bed and declared this was her baby.

Randy was hanging by the door. Mom called him over.

"You've got a little brother," she said, handing the baby to him, and we all peered at the baby's face. It wasn't scrunched up. His skin was pure as a cloud, his hair was golden white. He was about the most beautiful thing I'd ever seen.

"We'll call him David," Mom said.

It was a pretty easy birth so Mom only had to stay another night. The nurses figured out our situation and brought in extra breakfast trays for us to share. Then our whole litter slept on a couch in the waiting room.

On the drive home, Randy took his job of big brother seriously, protecting David in his arms, buffering the bumps, and bracing his legs against the front seat.

After a few months or so, Mom started working part-time again, with Randy and I trading off staying home to babysit. This is when Randy really started to get angry over Dad's absence. He would say things like, "Why doesn't Dad come home and help?" I missed Dad too, but I didn't miss the fighting.

One day in early spring, I came home from school to see Blackie Jenkins' pickup truck in our driveway. He was a logger and part Indian like Dad, a guarantee of defectiveness in Mom's book, but he didn't have the alcohol affliction and was always polite. It was an event just to have a visitor and he'd brought a surprise: a twenty-four volume set of Encyclopedia Britannica, leather bound and brand new, in a dark wooden case, with a giant atlas that fit in the back.

"From your old man," Blackie winked. "He wants you to be smart."

The tired scowl on Mom's face was compounded by the

bawling baby in her arms. Our living room was bare, everything had gone up for collateral—a term I understood to mean a sacrifice people make to stay in their house. It was just like Dad to spend his paycheck on something wonderful rather than something essential.

"Where is our dad?" Randy asked.

The last time Blackie saw Dad he was heading off for Ramsay Arm, up by Desolation Sound. I wondered if this gift was a trade-off for never coming back. The books were big and sturdy and full of information, like Dad at his best. I could open one and read about the Parthenon and the Acropolis. I didn't have to go to the library anymore to see pictures of the Taj Mahal.

Ramsay Arm wasn't in the atlas so I put an X in the vicinity and some weeks later, like voodoo, the X'ed map appeared on the front page of the Fraser Valley News.

"Sea of Mud Slides Over B.C. Logging Camp. Three Dead."

At Brynel's Café on Old Yale Road, where an unpaid bill was festering, Mom persuaded Mrs. Brynel to let her use the phone because ours was disconnected.

On the newsstand, there was a photograph showing the entire camp buried in mud, broken bunkhouses, and trailers half sunk in the ocean. In the background a mammoth debris flow spewed down the denuded mountain.

The camp was a gyppo operation. Companies like this were always going belly-up before paychecks were issued. Mom was trying to contact the accountant, determined to get what Dad was owed.

It turned out the accountant was one of the casualties. The

company had no idea of Dad's whereabouts, or if his last cheque was claimed, but they said he wasn't one of the bodies they'd dug up.

Days went by. Another body was found. A survivor took a turn for the worse and died.

No word from Dad. I read up on mudslides in the encyclopedia. There were images of homes destroyed and little kids looking like they were sleeping under a blanket of chocolate, their nostrils blocked.

A few Saturdays later, I was sitting on Cheryl's bed singing, "She loves you yeah, yeah, yeah," when I was overwhelmed by a clear sense of knowing.

"My dad's home," I said, and ran.

Blackie's truck was in the driveway. Dad's muddy caulk boots and gunnysack were on the porch. He was holding court at the table, chuckling about the poor bugger who got crushed in his bunk. "He was just trying to sneak a few more hours sleep. He won't try that again. *Har har.*"

The kitchen was filled with the smell of a venison roast, courtesy of Blackie. Baby David was sitting up in Mom's lap, fascinated by the waving dirt-cracked hands and jolly voice of this storyteller he'd never met.

"Why did it happen?" Randy asked. He was standing right close to Dad, looking very serious.

Dad took a long breath in and blew out with his lips pursed. "Well, because we were over-logging. We stripped the whole hillside of trees. Then we had a week of hard rain. It was bound to happen. And the camp was right below. Don't shit where you eat. You know what I'm saying?"

"Why'd you do it then? Why'd you cut down so many trees?"
Dad shook his head, "Cause I'm not the boss."
"You should be."
Dad cracked a small smile. "Oh you think so, huh?"
I wondered why Dad would never be a boss.
A look passed between Mom and Dad, it wasn't anything to inspire The Beatles, but there was some kind of love in it.

Then Misty showed up and the peaceful mood between Mom and Dad changed. Our trip to Dad's parents earlier had precipitated a series of whispered fights. I couldn't hear the words being said but they sounded mean and angry. One night I heard a kerfuffle and Mom yelled out "Goddamn effing Christ!" and ran into the bathroom. I could hear Misty saying, "I'm sorry, Simone, I'm really sorry! Are you alright?"

I snuck downstairs and saw Mom in the bathroom dabbing blood from her nose. Misty turned to me and snapped, "It was an accident. Get to bed."

In the morning Dad's work gear was gone from the porch, which meant he was gone too.

Mom and Misty would find a way to get along, I guess out of necessity. Mom was working most of the time, so Misty would look after the baby.

We never observed birthdays, but Misty found out I was turning ten and called a party. She baked a cake and cooked hot dogs. I remember Mom and Misty sitting on the floor in the living room, laughing and drinking clear liquor. Lemon gin comes to mind. That's the only time I've ever seen Mom drink. She was all blue and green under her eyes where the swelling from Misty's punch had gone down and she was acting like a crazy cat.

Cheryl's mother fetched her early.

I had one other friend, Cornelia. Her family were Mennonites who'd left the community. She was a pale, almost blue-skinned girl with white hair and round, wire-rimmed glasses. She looked and acted like an old lady, maybe that's why I liked her. I was the only person she'd invited to her birthday. All the furniture in her home was wooden, built by her dad, a tall, broad-shouldered man with intolerant blue eyes and big hands. All the girls and women in her family looked like different versions of each other. Her grandmother only spoke German. That day, we sat at a long table drinking freshly pressed cherry juice and eating turkey sandwiches on home-baked bread, and everyone said nice things about Cornelia.

Now she was sitting on our living room floor reading through an encyclopedia, ignoring the cuckooness around her. That's when from the open door a bushy creature streaked into the living room. It was a squirrel, not a rat. Everyone was screaming and laughing, making the squirrel frantic. They had it cornered so I took a paper grocery bag, pounced on it, and scooped it up. As I was carrying it outside, the squirrel bit through the bag into my thumb. It was bloody and painful. Cornelia said I should get a rabies shot because squirrels can be rabid and I might go crazy with hydrophobia.

When Cornelia's father came to pick her up, I tried to head him off at the back door, but he walked through the mess in our kitchen into the squalor of our living room. He introduced himself. Mom didn't even stand up, she just waved to him. Misty sniggered.

I knew Cornelia would not be coming back.

I looked up rabies in the encyclopedia and for weeks, every time a water tap went on, Randy would say "hydrophobia" in a spooky voice and bug out his eyes.

Mom cautioned us to stay out of the barns on our property because she said they were dangerous. That should have made exploring them irresistible but the multitude of rats running around was a big deterrent for me. In one of the buildings, the roof had completely sunk to the floor and was being reclaimed by quickweed and thistles. The other barn had a pile of rusted machine parts and broken objects piled in the center. It looked like someone had just ploughed them into a heap and given up. One day Mr. Person asked if he could look through everything and Mom told him he could take whatever he wanted.

While he was loading up his pick-up truck, I spotted a beat-up banjo that he'd leaned against the barn. I didn't ask, I just took it for myself. I didn't know, but it was a left-hander. Its strings were dead so I tightened them up until they emitted a kind of tone. From watching *Don Messer's Jubilee* on TV, I knew you held the neck in your left hand, so I actually played the banjo upside-down. I invented open chords that had some semblance of music, and I made up songs about being broken hearted. "God, Where Did You Go?" I still believed there was a God. We just weren't on his radar.

Randy and I looked after Marlene and Kate when Mom was working. Cheryl's mom started taking the baby. She had thick glasses over a crinkled nose, and it looked like she was always saying "Huh?" She called me Barb. "Is your mom home yet, Barb? Well I'm just gonna take the little ones home with me. Tell her to come by in the morning, Barb."

Sunday nights we had a bath and washed our hair before the school week began. We had to share the same water because our hot water tank wasn't big. We rotated who got to go first. A hot clean bath by myself was my biggest pleasure after having to sit in other people's grime.

Even with the detangler Tame my hair was a mess of knots. We'd sit watching the *Ed Sullivan Show* while Mom yanked my hair smooth. It hurt but it was also a tenderness. I loved the cozy ritual with the baby in his crib, Randy on the floor and my sisters nestled in his lap. I would never sit on the floor because of the rat I saw run over Randy's legs one time.

In the week after President Kennedy died, the television was on constantly. We were sent home from school even though we were Canadian. Then we watched the image of Lee Harvey Oswald getting shot over and over, and each time I was horrified and fascinated by the expression on his face.

Our most wonderful TV night ever was when The Beatles played on *Ed Sullivan*. Mom made sweet cocoa and popcorn with real butter. We all gathered while they were introduced. When Paul opened his mouth, "Oh please, say to meeeee . . ." I got shivers. He looked like a naughty angel. I couldn't sit down. I danced in the center of the living room emoting like an opera singer as I sang every word. Randy sat drumming on the floor, not quite as excited as me, but he still chimed in for the chorus, "I wanna hold your haaaand, I wanna hold your hand." It thrilled me to think of all the people watching. Television was the great equalizer.

People Gather

Mom is standing looking out the window at some far away memory. Bobby, Paul, and Kate, the three giants, are squeezed shoulder to shoulder on the sofa, while Red kneels over one of Dad's navigation maps on the floor. "This was all primo logging area," he says, sweeping his hand over the map. "Vancouver was thick with Douglas firs and red cedars. It used to be Salish Indian land for nine thousand years. Europeans brought smallpox and that pretty much wiped them out. But, you know, a lot of those Natives you see on the street, face down on the cement, they are the original people."

Then Paul asks, "So when did people build all those scuzzy hotels?"

"The first hotels were built for workers. They weren't considered scuzzy. The bars on the first floor were like offices for loggers. That's where your father and I used to pick up our work. You know what corduroy skids are?"

The kids all shake their heads no.

"They were roads made of logs covered with sand. Pack

horses would skid logs along the road to Hastings Mill or Burrard Inlet," says Red. "See here? This is where they would be dumped, turned into booms, and towed away." Red traces his finger along the Inlet. "That's why they called it Skid Road. It was not a desirable place to live and of course loggers tend to over-reward themselves with alcohol, so it became known as a workers' slum. It got scuzzy when the drugs came. Opium. That happened when Chinese men were brought over as indentured servants. They were all housed on Skid Road because of the Asian exclusion laws. You know about that?"

The kids don't know.

"You'd be surprised what a racist history we have. The Chinese were brought over to build the railway under horrible conditions. Good white people didn't want them living in their neighborhoods so they created laws to keep them out. Skid Road was the only place they could go. That's why you've got Chinatown running side-by-side with it. The Chinese kept to themselves, you know, they always looked after their own, but they brought opium, and it seeped into the logging haunts. Then you've got all those hardworking men in one place longing for some female company. Of course no upstanding woman would be seen on Skid Road, so, well . . . You know where that goes."

Mom sighs, unaware that she can be heard. Her face is dropping, her eyes forgetting, like a sleeping horse. If there was a bed next to her I would tip her over and cover her up.

Red shifts so he's sitting with his back against the wall. His voice gets softer.

"What really brought down Skid Road was the invention

of the hypodermic needle. They went from smoking opium to shooting up. Prostitutes became addicts and sold their wares to feed the habit. That's a snake eating its tail. Skid Road at some point got called Skid Row, the place to go when you're hitting the skids."

"And the reputation of loggers hit the skids too," Dad says with a sort of mock indignity.

There's a loud bang on the door. Mom comes out of her daze and retreats to the bathroom, just as Jack M. walks in.

"Speak of the devil," Dad says.

Jack is big and loud and always sweating. He's Dad's most constant companion, a logger and no stranger to Skid Row.

"Hey, Barb," he says, giving me a hearty pat on my shoulder. "Hi, kids," he says and sits on the edge of the sofa. "I'm so sorry. It's rotten, just so rotten. I feel so bad for ya." He puts an arm around Bobby, "How ya doin', pal?" and Bobby starts to well up.

The kids like Jack. I used to like him. I thought he was a great guy and a good father. He was always playing catch with us and taking us swimming. Then one day he took my hard-earned tape recorder to be fixed and never returned it. Dad said, "Oh that went right up his arm," which I didn't understand at the time. He's a heroin addict and thief. His wife, Bev, just seemed like a regular housewife who nagged a lot, until I saw her in a public pool and Dad pointed out the prison tattoos on her shoulders. Bev died recently of a heart attack. Jack is just back from a short stint in jail for robbing an A&W drive-in. He says he didn't plan to do it. He'd gone in the back to use the phone and saw a bag sitting on a stool, which he correctly presumed was cash. Jack says, "I can resist anything but temptation." He took the bag and sped off but the waitress had written down his license plate number when she took his order. The police were waiting for him when he got home.

The whole crew travels to a spaghetti restaurant to meet Dad's brother Bill who has flown in from Toronto. He's only seen Dad twice in the last thirty years, at their mother's funeral, then at their father's a year later. Now it's Randy's turn. In spite of his parent's vilification of Dad, and their polar opposite politics, Bill seems to like him. Misty is perched beside Uncle Bill with her arms around her knees. The bottom of her long skirt is shredded and muddy, and she smells like pot and patchouli. Bill was five when Dad left, and ten when his father brought Dad's kids home, so he's close to them. He tells Dad that Dana sends her condolences. I guess he keeps in touch with her. I know she has gone very cold on Dad.

The kids all huddle at the end of the table and Dad sneaks a little beer into their glasses.

"How are you, Misty?" Red asks.

She shakes her head like she's doing all she can to bear the pain. Red's fond of her. I remember hearing him tell Mom that Misty was a "knock-out" and "highly intelligent." Even though he's certain most of her stories are fiction, it impresses him all the more.

I bring up the play I'll be doing in Toronto, just for something to say.

"Well, come stay with us," Uncle Bill says. "You can catch a streetcar on the corner that goes right up to the Tarragon Theatre."

I tell him the theater will give me housing, skipping the detail that rehearsals started yesterday.

Colleen arrives, my only childhood friend I still know. She hugs me. Her family came from California and they're not awkward about hugging.

At first everyone is low key, expressing condolences to Mom, but because no one is inclined to speak about why we're all here, the conversation veers into politics.

Colleen is even further left than Dad—"If Bill Bennett had his way, he'd cut every social program that's worth anything," she says.

"At least he's kind to small businesses," says Uncle Bill. Bill runs a BP gas station and owns real estate. He has a Chinese wife who escaped China after her family was killed during the Cultural Revolution. She keeps his books. Bill believes in free enterprise.

"The Social Credit are ruining labor," Colleen tells them. "I wish Dave Barrett was still in office."

"You know he's a good friend of mine?" brags Jack M.

"Isn't he your probation officer?" Dad jibes.

"Ya, ya, but he's a friend too."

"If only the NDP could win the federal election," says Colleen.

"Oh Jesus!" Uncle Bill exclaims. "Ed Broadbent would have school kids singing the Communist anthem. What's it called?"

"The Internationale," Red says.

"Better than God Save the Queen," Colleen snaps.

I wish everyone would just stop talking and do something brave like hold hands and contemplate what's happened.

Mom is staring into the wood grain of the table.

"Trudeau is not a loyalist," Red interjects. "Some of his ideas are socialist."

"He believes everyone should have an equal place at the table," Dad says, "just not his table."

"Exactly, he's a total elitist," says Colleen.

"Simone likes him *par ce qu'il est vraiment beau et très charmant*," Dad adds, exaggerating a Québecois accent. The table goes silent for a moment as Mom lifts her head to speak.

"It doesn't matter to me who's Prime Minister," she says. "It makes no difference in my life."

Kate waves to me from the end of the table where she sits with Bobby and Paul. She seems like a good person. I think we both appreciate that we don't need each other. Bobby doesn't need me either.

Marlene needs a lifeline, but I'm not up to the task.

Jack M. brings an acquaintance to the table. The guy's had a few drinks but he's steady.

"Hi, Jack," he reaches out a hand that is missing two fingers. "I just wanted to say, I'm really sorry about your son."

Dad takes in a breath and nods uncomfortably. He shakes the guy's hand for a moment, then he holds it up. "Now this guy's had bad luck!" Dad says, displaying the missing digits, then he picks up the other hand. Three more fingers are missing. "I mean really bad luck."

The guy is passive, embarrassed more by Dad's behavior than his maimed hands.

"It's just a terrible thing for a child to die before his parents," he says.

Dad can't respond. He taps a cigarette on the table.

The guy turns to Mom. "Hi. Simone, is it? We met when Jack and I were selling peavey sticks on the Sunshine Coast."

Mom nods. Its not clear if she remembers.

"That was a helluva fire season. Summer of '67," Dad says, lighting his cigarette and turning away from the guy. "You remember Red? Or maybe you were floating down the Ganges that summer."

"Very sorry for your loss." The guy puts his better hand on Mom's hand. She stares at it, mouths thank you, and he leaves.

"Got both hands stuck in a winch line and no one could turn it off," Dad says. "Up in Jarvis Inlet. That was a real suicide show."

"Jack." Mom stops him.

"He was a good logger though."

Mom is starting to look ghostly and I need air. I suggest we walk back to the Ryan Street house.

Mom floats up and out the door. I follow a few steps behind.

It's turned chilly outside. "Are you okay?" I call out. A ridiculous question.

She nods her head but doesn't turn, just moves down the sidewalk with long strides. Her arms dangle and swing like Granddad's. She always walks in time, always in a rush. Like Randy, Mom is most herself when she's moving. "Do you remember when you taught me how to skip?" I say. She doesn't respond, but I know she hears me. "It was in Bear Creek, walking home from the beach." That day, I was cold and shivering. She told me to lift my foot, to hop up on the other one, then slide forward. I couldn't get the knack. She grabbed my wrist. "Hop up and slide," she said, "like this, see—hop and slide." I hopped and faltered, she bobbed and glided. My foot was still shy from the braces and just wouldn't fall in place: my eternal reticence. I'd rather stay behind than stumble in uncertainty, but Mom's grip got stronger and she pulled me on. "Hop and slide, hop and slide, hop and slide," she said, over and over, until my body stopped trying and my foot forgot its shyness, the rhythm got inside me, and I was skipping. I was skipping! I skipped down the dirt road all the way home.

After a long silence, Mom says, "That's how my mother taught me, to warm me up when we were coming home from the lake." I think of her mother's hands, which I know from Granddad's photographs. I think of my grandmother's big hand around Mom's tiny wrist, pulling her forward, and of Mom's hand around my wrist, pulling me forward, skipping through the cold.

Dad and Misty left us kids waiting in the car while they went into a Hastings Street hotel bar. It had been light when we parked, now it was dark on Skid Row. I tried to make out shapes through the bar's blackened windows. A bent-nosed face stuck a rotten mouth up to our slightly opened window. "You kids all alone?" the man slurred, trying to pretend he could be of help. I shielded the baby from his breath.

Randy said, "Go in there and ask for Jack Williams."

"Jack Williams, sure, sure," the drunk man said, mustering some purpose, but then he tripped on the stairs of the hotel and sat down, forgetting where he was.

Dad would always say something like, "I'm just going to find out what time I leave on Monday." This time he said he was getting his caulk boots from Red, but we'd seen Red leave hours ago.

Randy got out of the car and pushed open the doors of the hotel for the second time that night. He came out being shoved ahead by Dad. Dad wasn't mean, alcohol just made him act badly. He never hit but he would shove. He walked like he was on a raft in a squamish, holding up a beer. I hoped he'd let Randy steer the car, but he pushed him aside and started it up. Misty came wiggle-waggling down the steps. She liked people looking at her. She stood in front of the car and mouthed a shriek, like she was about to be run over. Then she opened the door and pushed Randy into the middle.

Randy secretly passed Dad's bottle of beer to me and I poured it out the window, like I always did. Dad drove the way he walked, staggering, leaning to one side, almost losing his balance, then regaining it by tipping over to the other side.

Randy watched the road in a kneeling position, ready to grab the wheel if he could. I pretended we were in a cartoon, convincing myself that if we crashed there would be no pain and the baby would fly out the window and land on a cushy tree top. We'd do multiple flips over the concrete and come to rest on lily pads in a swamp. We arrived nose-to-nose with the back porch. Misty slept on the front seat. Dad reached the kitchen floor to pass out safely.

All the ill feeling I had toward Misty crystallized one day. She was supposed to be minding us while Mom was at work, but she only really cared about the baby. She loved that baby. On this day, she had some guys over and we were annoying her, so she locked us out of the house.

I stuck a piece of rubber hose through an open window and yelled stupid things. She came roaring out and chased me across the highway into the neighbor's open garage. With one good shove, I fell against a work bench and knocked over a can of paint.

Marine-blue enamel spread across the cement floor and saturated my backside. I sulked home and climbed through Mom's bedroom window, trying not to smear her bed in blue. I was wearing only underwear and paint, trying to find clothes to change into, when this guy came in. He was Native, about twenty, I'll call him DD—he has the same name as a West Coast artist, otherwise I'd out him. I went into the closet and pulled on one of my mom's pregnancy muumuus.

When I came out he was lying on the bed and told me to come lie beside him. He was like a dog with crazy eyes. I didn't make any sudden moves for fear he'd pounce. I sat on the edge of the bed facing away, trying to slow my breathing and to keep the muumuu from slipping off my shoulders. "Have you ever seen a guy sing?" is what I heard. I'd seen The Beatles sing on *The Ed Sullivan Show*, I told him. He laughed through his nose, "A guy's thing. Thing!"

The window was still wide open. I saw myself diving through, then I was tumbling on the grass.

The four-year-old was making mud pies in the front yard. I couldn't see Marlene. I grabbed Kate and circled around the house, then hauled her across the highway where Randy was playing catch with the neighbor kid whose garage was marked by a trail of blue footprints. Marlene wasn't with Randy. Then I saw DD skittering away from the house like a coyote with a rabbit in his mouth. We all ran to the house calling for Marlene. She didn't answer. We found her upstairs cringing with shame as she put her pants back on.

Mom came home. The police were called. We were on a party line and Mom kept saying, "Please get off the line," but everyone was listening. From the stairwell I heard the police talking about how traumatic it would be for Marlene if they brought the man up on charges. I didn't know what traumatic meant. I guessed it was something similar to "dramatic," going to the city, talking in front of strangers. I could hear Mom sighing. We didn't have the resources for therapy, there weren't any pastors or trusted family doctors for Marlene to talk to. She just went silent, and after that the smallest things would upset her, she'd lash out and scratch you in the face.

When Dad came back from camp, things got worse between Misty and Mom, partly because Dad seemed to favor Misty. She read books and made clever comments. We'll never get it straight how old she was. She looked the part enough to get into beer parlors with Dad, while Mom stayed home with us.

A few weeks later, us kids were driving with Dad when we passed a carload of teenagers.

"That's him!" Randy said. "That's DD!"

Dad did a U-turn and followed the car into a liquor store parking lot. The teenagers were pooling their money to buy booze when Dad stepped up to the car with Randy right behind him.

"Is that DD?" Dad asked the driver.

One of the guys said, "What do you want old man?" though Dad was only thirty-five. A few of the guys made punky remarks, but Dad silenced them. "He molested a seven-year-old girl."

The guys then watched as Dad grabbed DD and hauled him from the back seat of the car. He slapped him several times, threw him down, and gave his head one good crack on the concrete. His friends sped off in their car. Randy stood over the limp body, looking at the blood pooling under his head.

"Get in the car," Dad yelled.

Revenge didn't feel good. It's just something that had to be done. It didn't help anybody. Randy sat up front, staring sideways at Dad like he was a killer worthy of respect. Marlene pushed her head into the back of the driver's seat and looked at her lap. It's hard to know how many of Marlene's problems relate to those events. She's dyslexic but still did well in school. She had to work really hard and would have panic attacks over numbers and letters, though now she earns her money bookkeeping. Being tall and pretty brought her a circle of friends through her teens.

Years later, when she was in her early twenties, she was going to the planetarium in Vancouver with some friends, and there, taking tickets, was DD. She knew it was him. He didn't recognize her, of course. She said he seemed very off and wondered if Dad's beating might have caused a brain injury. This seems to be the point Marlene started to self-medicate.

Box of Treasures

Back at Ryan Street, I'm feeling Randy strongly right now, he's challenging me. I'm afraid of heights but if he jumped off a cliff I would follow. He once branded his arm with an iron. I outdid him. I let him hold the iron down on the inside of my forearm for several seconds, and I still have a brown iron-shaped scar with little circles for the steam holes.

Now he's challenging me to face the room where he died. I'm guessing Mom didn't open the window because there's a powerful smell of disinfectant emanating from inside. I crack the door. The little cot with a grey flannel blanket is unmade. Metal venetian blinds are closed. On the small dresser beside the bed is a metal ashtray coated with ashes.

Mom's light is off but I know she's awake, I can feel her thoughts writhing in the dark.

I give up and go back to the chocolate box, to crinkled photographs of Mom's family from when she was little. She's like a scrawny kitten. Tinker is blonde and radiant, destined for California. The middle sister, Mary, is more plain. I'm mesmerized by this proof of Mom's childhood. My grandmother has a strong body and those big hands. I used to think her face was so beautiful, but after I found out she was a suicide, I could only see her suffering. Granddad's face and physique are my idea of perfect. His body is lean and muscular, and he has a wide forehead above even features. There's nothing excessive about him.

I remember the day I came home from school to find a big box sitting in the center of our living room. Inside were these photographs, along with a treasure trove of Granddad's possessions.

I remember every item wrapped in newspaper and cushioned in shredded strips of more newspaper. I wonder if Granddad packed everything before he died. That would be in character, to leave no loose ends. On top was a leather pouch of Player's tobacco, with a shriveled apple peel inside, still keeping the tobacco moist two years later. A hunting knife in a leather case had a razor-sharp blade, narrowed from years of honing, and a handle of wood and bone. I'd seen it hanging from Granddad's belt. There was a rough tweed suit with leather patches on the elbows, and an archery set with real arrows. Randy and I would use our chickens as targets and would end up having to pluck and gut them.

There were three paintings. I recognized the one of Lake Louise because Granddad told me it was the same Alpine-blue color of his car. One painting showed a boat on the shore of the Whirlpool River. I knew that because

Mom told me about the big rock they used to swim to. Then there was a landscape of a mountain thick with evergreens, under an azure sky and titanium clouds. The colors were all described in notebooks, with each element of each painting alphabetically indexed. S=Sky: 2 pts azure blue, C = clouds: titanium white. Cloud shadows: titanium with dab of black. T= Tree foliage: equal parts royal blue and cadmium yellow.

There was an incomplete canvas with a grid drawn in pencil underneath a sketch of snow-capped mountains. The Rockies.

Wrapped in a light suede shammy were his brushes, the microscopic layers of embedded paint at their bases belying their youthful-looking bristles. In a wooden case, which I'm sure he made himself, were rows of oil paints in varying degrees of fullness. Each end was meticulously rolled, the way Granddad showed me how to roll up a tube of toothpaste. This was sacred stuff. And all of it had disappeared now, most likely given away by Dad, everything but the photographs.

The Orca's Curse

It was a terrible winter, freakishly cold. A Haida woman being interviewed on the radio said the cold weather would not break until the Vancouver aquarium released a killer whale they had in captivity. An artist had harpooned the whale off Saturna Island to use it as a model for a giant sculpture he was commissioned to make. But it didn't die. He shot it and it still didn't die, so the aquarium director towed it back to Vancouver and put it on display. They called it Moby Doll.

We took our first train ride to Vancouver looking for Dad. It was a long walk through frozen streets from the station to downtown, and we weren't dressed for it. Randy carried baby David all the way, holding him inside his jacket. When Kate started crying because her feet were cold, Mom carried her. We came to Eaton's department store and ducked inside. It was warm, and there was Christmas music playing and a giant twinkling tree in the foyer. After we'd all used the toilet and luxuriated under the hand drier—about the niftiest invention I'd seen—we were sent down to wait by the tree. Mom went off with Marlene.

I could have stared at the colored lights playing on tinsel all day but suddenly Mom was whisking us out the door. "Where's Marlene?" Randy asked her.

"It's okay," she said, herding us down the sidewalk. She stopped outside a little magazine shop and lit a cigarette. "Go get some gum and wait in there." She gave us some change and again we took refuge in the warmth inside. After we had loitered for several minutes—with Kate grabbing bars of chocolate off the shelf, saying "mine," and the baby screaming for a bottle—the man behind the counter told us it was time to go.

Mom wasn't outside. There was a police car in front of Eaton's and somehow I knew it had to do with Mom. We walked back to see her sitting in the front seat with a policeman, Marlene cowering in the back. Another man in a suit jacket was standing outside the car trying to shake off the cold. He looked us over. "Is that your mother in there?" he said.

Randy and I both nodded. The baby was still wailing. Kate was biting my hand.

The man shook his head and knocked on the cop's window. The cop got out and, after a little conference with the suited man, he opened the car door and let Mom and Marlene go.

Marlene was wearing a coat, brand new with the tags still on.

"Okay, we're not going to do that again are we?"

He was looking at Marlene but talking to Mom. Somehow Mom had managed to put lipstick on since I'd last seen her. She slipped the coat off a mute Marlene and handed it to the suited man. "No, it won't happen again," she said, thanking him with her eyes.

The cop had no meanness in his voice. I could see he kind of liked Mom. "Well, get where you're going and stay out of the cold."

After more numb-footed, chatter-teeth walking, we found Dad at an apartment. He was staying with a woman named Hazel who ran an old folks home on the first floor. She seemed older than Dad and was not pretty at all. She had backcombed, hay-like hair, a big sloppy bust, a potbelly, and legs with no meat on them. She put her Cameo cigarettes in a holder and took deep long drags. When she exhaled, she'd make some clever quip that only she and Dad understood. We sat in the lobby around a fountain while Hazel and Dad joked about how the sound of the running water made the old folks wet their pants.

This woman couldn't have been more different than Mom, and Randy glowered at her the entire time. We finally ditched her and walked down Hastings Street, still freezing but no one complained. We didn't want to upset the calm between Mom and Dad. We passed the Patricia Hotel bar and were relieved when Dad only looked through the window without breaking stride. We ducked into a crack-a-joke shop and had a huge laugh when Mom gagged at fake vomit Dad set in front of her.

At the Only Seafood Chinese restaurant, Randy and I stood by the aquarium watching lobsters with bound claws unable to fight their fate. When we sat down, Dad showed us how to dip our fingers in soy sauce then roll them in sesame seeds to make a sesame popsicle. He asked if we wanted to see a lobster boiled alive and we all screamed "No!"

The seven of us squeezed into a booth and played roulette with the lazy Susan. Whatever dish landed in front of us, chow-mein or spring rolls, everything was good. Under the red paper lanterns, amid the loud din of strangers talking, it was a moment of plenty for us.

Then we went back to Hazel's and slept on the carpet.

In the morning we caught a bus to the train station. Mom and Dad sat together, quietly talking and staring out the window. I loved seeing them sit so close together, holding my baby brother while he slept.

At the station, Dad bought us each an orange pop. It wasn't until we were boarding that I realized he wasn't coming home with us. Dad and Mom nodded to each other. Randy kept his head down and got on the train. I said goodbye and tried not to cry.

There was a black porter on the train. I had never seen a black person before. We had only once driven by a black man riding a bicycle on the side of the highway. He was tall and skinny, with a long coat billowing behind him, but he disappeared into the distance. I admired the porter for hours. Every time he walked by, he would smile and make me smile, in spite of how bad I was feeling. Dad talked about how black people in the United States weren't allowed in some schools and restaurants, public bathrooms or pools, and that President Kennedy had been working on a law to change that before he was killed. On TV, I'd seen Shirley Temple dancing down the stairs with Bojangles. I'd heard a black choir in *The Green Pastures*. I waved to the porter and asked him if he could open my pop. He stuck the bottle top in his mouth and snapped the cap off with his molars.

We got home to find the house frigid and the water wouldn't turn on. We'd run out of oil for the stove. Mr. Person told Mom the pipes were frozen, and if she turned the stove on, the pipes would crack. Someone would have to get under the house with heaters to slowly melt the pipes. He didn't know where she could get those kind of heaters.

We all went to bed. Mom woke me in the dark of morning to say she had to take the baby to the hospital. His eardrums had ruptured from the cold, but I would find that out much later. She said that Dad was on his way and I should stay home to look after Kate until he arrived. Randy went to school with Marlene.

Dad didn't come. The next day, Mom wasn't back and Dad still hadn't shown up, so Randy stayed home and I took Marlene to school.

A few more days passed. I began to hang my hopes on the killer whale. If they'd just release Moby Doll, this bad spell would end. At Byrnel's Cafe, the truck stop and grocery store across the highway, we asked for food on credit, with the usual line that Mom would be getting her check at the end of the week. Mrs. Byrnel was a white-haired woman with a pleasing face, kind and sympathetic. Her husband was grumpy like Fred Mertz in *I Love Lucy*. I was afraid to ask him for anything, so I'd wait outside until I saw Mrs. Brynel standing behind the counter. She gave me bread and eggs. I walked home planning what I would do with the eggs. We didn't have any butter to fry them, but there was little bit of mayonnaise in the fridge so I figured I could boil them and make deviled eggs. I got home and filled a pot with water, then I remembered we didn't have any heat. I stood at the cold stove wondering what I should do. Randy said, "I know." He scooped an egg out, held it up like he was examining it, then cracked it open on my head. I immediately retaliated with an egg torpedo cracked on his back. He grabbed the half-full carton, I grabbed the pot of eggs in the cold water, and the war was on. We ran around the house bombing each other, slipping on yolks, splattering the walls, and making a terrible mess until our ammo was depleted. Then we ate peanut butter sandwiches for two days.

We would never ask for charity from our neighbors, since our Granddad would have rolled in his grave. We had a tab at Byrnel's, and Mom would eventually pay it, but the next time I went, Mrs. Brynel got that "Oh dear" look when she saw me coming. She gave me a tin of stewed tomatoes and shooed me out the door before her husband could see.

That night, her offering went down with the kids like a tin of stewed tomatoes.

After a while, Mrs. Brynel wouldn't even say anything when I came foraging. She'd just slip a can of beans and some bread in a bag and put her head down until I left. Once her husband came out and yelled, "Where's your mother?" and while I stood there trying to come up with the right answer my bladder released. Pee went down my legs in my pants, into my socks and shoes, to form a little puddle beneath me.

"Did you have an accident, dear?" Mrs. Byrnel asked. I didn't understand what she meant by accident.

"No, I peed my pants." I said, cringing out the door with the beans and bread.

Under a dark sky, the snow had turned to ice and its crust was like broken glass cutting into my ankles. By the time I walked across the highway and down the driveway, my pants were frosted. Our house was an iceberg. There was no hot water to clean myself with. I was walking in stiff-legged circles, then Randy saw me and started laughing. I told him what happened and then we both busted a gut. Then it happened again—I thawed out my frozen pants with more warm pee. And then I started to feel strange, my back hurt, and I was shivering. The next little while is a blur. I remember Mrs. Person came over and took me to the doctor in Chilliwack. And Marlene and Kate stayed with her.

I was sent to stay down the road with the Brook family. They had a nice piece of property with a long driveway with two entrances. They had a corral and a little stable for their daughter's black and white pony. Their daughter was a whiny girl, also named Barbara, so they called me Babs. I was not allowed to go near Barbara's pony. She was younger than I was, but she read a lot and felt a need to stick her nose into my exercise books to point out my mistakes. We had twin beds but were not equals.

Mrs. Brook was a blank, but Mr. Brook was rotund and red-faced, always in a huff. After one service at their church, I was done. Not one word of the sermon made sense: "Verily this and that. God knoweth all things." At first it made me mad and then it made me sleepy. The next Sunday I didn't want to go to church and Mr. Brook said I had to. When I told him I hated God, he slapped me across the face.

The orca developed a skin disease because the harbor wasn't salty enough. Then it died. The bus would pass our house on the way to school. All our belongings were stacked in a pile on the front yard, growing moldy like a skin disease. I wanted to die too.

The cold spell broke but Mom still hadn't shown up. I'd had a toothache for a while that I'd been keeping to myself, but one morning I couldn't lift my head. My jaw swelled up huge, and Mrs. Brook insisted that her husband take the bus to work so she could drive me to a dentist.

The dentist gave me gas and I woke up with no cares, until the middle of the night when I woke up feeling bad in every way. My jaw hurt, my head ached, and I was lonely for my mom. I thought I heard Mrs. and Mr. Brook whispering but it wasn't them. I looked over at the other Barbara, sleeping all cozy in her identical bed. I managed to yell "Hey!" and the voices stopped. Barbara woke up for a second and grumbled. I didn't take my eyes off her for the rest of the night. Somehow that anchored me.

Randy had hidden out in the house for a few days, then he got cornered on the roof by Mr. Person, who told him that if he didn't come down the police would bring him down. He was driven out to Chilliwack to stay with Chuck Ludivik's family. Chuck's parents and younger sister all wore glasses and liked to tell jokes, just like Chuck. They were always laughing and pulling pranks. At first Randy liked being there. He had his own room and felt important when Chuck drove him to school. Nobody knew him at school, so he wasn't embarrassed about our situation. Chuck called Randy his little cousin and treated him to burgers at A&W. He gave him a jackknife and an old baseball jacket that fit him perfectly. He always asked Randy if there was anything he needed. He even got him to talk about how he was feeling, something Randy never did. Then Randy started to resent being the object of someone's charity and began to shun Chuck. He closed his door and avoided being alone with him. He got up earlier, took the bus to school, then would run back after.

Around the end of the school year, I heard a rumbling outside and I sensed Dad was near. A big moving van was chugging down the Brook's long narrow driveway, snapping overhanging branches and kicking up dust. It lurched to a stop about an inch from the front porch. Mr. Brook was fuming, but he didn't say a word.

Dad stuck his head out the window and nodded to him.

"Okay, Barbara, get your gear," he shouted.

I don't know if Mr. and Mrs. Brook were expecting Dad—they hadn't said anything to me. Mr. Brook stood watch, making sure the truck didn't do any damage to his flower beds.

Mrs. Brook came out with my clothes in a pillow case. She put her hands on my shoulders and whispered, "I really hope things go better for you and your family, dear." It felt like the beginning of a relationship, just as it was ending. Then she gave me a brand new toothbrush and reminded me to brush twice a day.

"Cheerio," Dad said to Mr. Brook, in a smart-ass kind of way.

I squeezed into the cab and there was Randy, Marlene, and Kate. The girls had fleshed out a bit. Randy was a little taller and more mature looking. The most noticeable change was the awkwardness between us. No one wanted to talk about where we'd been, and we didn't know where we were going.

We checked into a motel just down the road. In the night, Mom and baby David showed up, except now the baby's name was Bobby. Mom was thinner and her peaches and cream complexion looked more pale parsnip. She has never talked about what happened or where she was when she went away, but she kept the baby all through it.

We caught the ferry to the very rainy Sunshine Coast. I guess we were starting a new life.

It was hot so we pulled over to take a swim at the first beach we saw. All I had to wear were a pair of oversized denim shorts and a padded swimsuit top that made me look like I had huge breasts when there was nothing there. I think they were clothes passed on from Hazel at the old folks home, maybe from the dead.

Randy plunged into the chilly water and swam out beyond the dock—out beyond the pilings, beyond the buoys, beyond the fishing boats, beyond where I could see him anymore. I walked to the end of the dock to spot him and a gaggle of girls swooped down on me, asking where I was from and how old I was. I wasn't from anywhere in particular, and in that moment I'd forgotten how old I was. Feeling the need to live up to my fake bust, I told them sixteen and jumped in the water. The padded top floated up to my neck and the girls started to whoop. I stayed there until everyone left, until Randy came back, until summer was over.

Another New Beginning

This is in Gibson's Landing. Dad befriended a photographer who took this picture. It's the only family picture Grand-dad didn't take. The guy put a white backdrop behind us and used a stuffed white rabbit to make us smile. I think we all look like good-natured little wolves. Bobby's about three, so I must be thirteen, Randy fourteen. We're wearing new clothes. Randy wore that corduroy shirt every day for two years. My hair is ironed straight. I'm wearing my first pair of earrings. It was Randy who pierced my ears by freezing them with an ice cube then sticking a sewing needle through the lobe into half a potato behind it.

We were the first tenants in an apartment building that was still being built. It was sterile and cheap, with asbestos ceilings and lead paint, I'm sure, but it was rodent-free. Since we had reunited, Mom was being meek and agreeable with Dad. Dad was sober and tense. He was booming up the inlet and came back every day.

The only thing worth keeping from our yard pile of

possessions was our arborite table, the encyclopedias, and my grandmother's old Singer sewing machine. Everything else of value was gone. Granddad's paintings, art supplies, and all his calligraphy pens and oil paints—gone.

Dad brought home a cheap guitar that someone had left in a camp cookhouse. Mom got me a Hank Williams songbook and I set about teaching myself to play on a right-handed stringed instrument, the right side up this time.

Our first next-door neighbors were a well-travelled old couple. The man played the oboe and introduced me to the music of Yma Sumac, who could sing five octaves. Mostly I liked to watch my neighbor's face as he played oboe along with her freaky high notes and subhuman low notes. He was keen to hear me sing, but after I strummed out "Lovesick Blues" he expressed no interest in hearing any more songs. I would still knock on his door to listen to the Incan princess and to eat cherry almond nougat from South Africa.

I don't know how Randy learned to be so good on the guitar, he just had natural ability. His fingers were longer and stronger than mine. I practiced until my hands ached and my digits bled. He picked it up and played licks from The Cream and Jimmy Hendrix with no effort. We played chess and, of course, he was better than I was. He tried to take me to a higher level but chess made me cold. I needed to move and make sound.

We had a fort in the woods behind the apartment buildings, a refuge from home and a place to escape in case of world disaster—the apocalypse or the rapture, we were in it together. It was also where I was initiated into smoking the Cameo cigarettes we stole from Mom.

Then the Fullers from California moved next door, replacing the Yma Sumac–loving oboe player. Colleen Fuller became my best friend. Her dad was a teacher and her mom was a librarian. They were civil rights activists who were hounded by the FBI and worried their youngest son might one day be drafted into the Vietnam War, so they immigrated to Canada. They became very involved with the Sechelt Reservation and created a class for Native kids. They had serious discussions at the dinner table about politics and books. One day, Mr. Fuller asked me what tribe Dad was from and I went mute. I still held the belief that you were only Indian if you lived on a reservation. I had no idea what tribe Dad was from.

Colleen and I sang Peter, Paul and Mary songs, playing the same parts on our guitars, with our ironed-straight hair and kohl-rimmed eyes. We clipped leaves from a marijuana plant Dad had growing on the balcony and baked them in the oven. I liked the lead-up to getting high, but the smoke made my brain come unglued. Then claustrophobia gripped me and I had to get outside and run.

Mr. Fuller knocked one day looking for Colleen and picked up a rollie on our floor. Dad knew he suspected the worst and didn't care, "It's tobacco Frank, I'd never be so careless with the good stuff."

Soon enough, Dad's sobriety wore off, along with Mom's tolerance. They were like B.C. weather—when the sun was out, there was nothing better, but when the gray socked in you lost the horizon and forgot the sun existed. They started to fight every night after Dad stumbled home from the legion hall. Mom would hurl a litany of complaints at him and he'd just mumble, trying to find a joke, which would make her fume. The fight usually ended with Mom throwing something that would break, and it felt like our family breaking one more time. Sometimes I'd hear her frustrated slaps against his chest. Her hands weren't capable of punching and Dad would never hit a woman, so the violence in their fights was more emotional than physical, more sad than angry.

One night I woke up thinking Mom was crying but the sound was too close, it was in my ears. Then I heard whispering, sneering, nattering. The voices were back. I tried to call out, but I couldn't move my mouth. I couldn't move my body. I shouted inside my head, "Go away!" The voices got louder and my inner shouting got louder too. I was gagged. Suffocating. Terrified. And then they stopped.

For months the voices hounded me. They'd jump me when I was about to fall asleep, or when I was walking on the trail from our fort in the woods. I was afraid to be alone, or to be awake when everyone was sleeping. I felt like I was being watched all the time. Mom took me to a doctor who said it might be growing pains, although I think he suspected I was taking drugs.

The voices, visitations, or whatever they were, all came to a head one night as I was slipping into sleep. I felt breathing on my eardrum, swearing around my neck, garbled words in a taunting tone, and the sensation of being pulled upward. Then a shout "Barbara!" My body was in a rigid cramp, screaming inside with no sound coming out. Marlene and Kate were asleep in the bed next to me. My body was being pulled upward with my feet still touching the bed, the blanket hung off me, and invisible eyes were all around. The voices were a current of wailing and weeping and giggling and swearing. All I could do was resist. My scream found passage. Then I fell to the floor. Marlene and Kate woke up. I went into Mom's room and she lay on her side listening to my description of what happened. She told me she didn't recognize me when I first came in. The voices never had any power over me after that night, but I believe that's when they got to Randy.

We were at Elphinstone High School now. From sewing classes in Home-Ec, I developed my flare for transforming ten-cent clothes I bought at the Women's Hospital Auxiliary into my look. I slimmed down fat-lady dresses and cut up men's sport coats.

Neither Randy or I did well academically. We weren't set up to do homework. We were distracted, tired, and unmotivated at school, but I was getting some breaks. I played guitar and sang in a church basement. I had a few friends.

Randy didn't make friends. One day he got into a hallway scuff with this older kid, I don't know why, and they both got the strap. After school, the guy and his sister started taunting us. She was on her bike, with a little gang around her. Randy just kept walking, but I turned around and started calling her names.

She rode up to me and sneered, "Where're you going, dearie?"

"Home darling," I said and rushed at her, pushing her and her bike into the ditch. I ran like hell, with all the kids chasing after me, back to the safety of the school grounds. But Randy walked right into a flurry of kicks and punches. When I saw that his nose was bleeding I started calling for help. The boys got a few more kicks in before Mr. "Monty" Montgomery drove up and they scattered. Mr. Montgomery was the vice principal and corporal punisher. He'd given me the strap earlier in the year for playing poker with three boys during recess. He rolled down his window and asked Randy if he was okay. Randy nodded, wiping his nose. He offered us a ride home, but Randy just walked away with me tailing after him.

When Dad got home, he looked at Randy's battered face and smiled.

The next day, Randy's nemesis and a few of his cohorts were called to the office and put on notice of expulsion if there were any more incidents. Randy was convinced he was at risk of a secret ambush and ran straight home after school. For the next several weeks, he played hooky until Mom was notified of his unexcused absences.

This is a drawing I did of Randy from a photograph. His troubles had set in but his mouth hadn't turned down yet. It seems like a good cover for the funeral brochure, the program, or whatever you call it. I try to think of something to write, but I'm just too dumb—numb, unsophisticated, raw, sad—to come up with something appropriate. Shakespeare's sonnet comes to mind, "Shall I compare thee to a summer's day?" only because I memorized it at theater school. It's not right, too lofty, not what Randy would want. But he wanted to be dead, how do you comply with that?

I find some pens in a drawer and start writing the sonnet in my finest calligraphy, thinking of Granddad. I see him in his cabin north of Lake Louise, where he always went when he wasn't working. I imagine him standing by an easel with a palette of shimmering oil paints, content and all-knowing. I see Randy with him, watching and learning.

When Randy started refusing to go to school, Mom pressured Dad to put in some father time. Dad figured learning to hunt was a good rite of passage for a teenager. He laid out his rifles and hunting gear on the living room floor and put us to work. It was unfamiliar to have this kind of attention from Dad and Randy wanted to show that he was worthy. Dad cleaned and oiled his 30/30 rifle, while Randy carefully honed the blade of the hunting knife.

"Short and sharp," Dad told him. "Then it's easier to guide it through the sinew and muscle without puncturing the intestines when you're field dressing."

I slipped the pointed little missiles into the rows of loops along Dad's vest, appalled that they might enter the flesh of an innocent animal.

"Best to get a clean shot to the heart," Dad said, positioning the rifle. "Get that deer in your sights, switch off the safety, *click*, *bang!*, the deer goes down. A shot like that clips the blood vessels, bleeds the muscles and makes for sweeter meat. A little higher cracks the spine, that's good too. Gut shots are bad. Deer run forever on adrenaline." We listened. "Whatever you do, do not pursue. If a deer runs after it's been shot the meat will go rigid. It'll drop on its own if you leave it alone. Then we gut it on the spot. You have to tie off the rectum and be careful cutting out the bladder. You don't want piss and shit messing up a good rump roast."

I imagine Randy and Dad driving up the peninsula listening to CBC news on Dad's shortwave radio. Dad prided himself on being informed and always carried his radio with him—on the boats, on the booms, and in bed. He would fall asleep listening to the classical music station. Randy was too intimidated to express opinions on world events. I'm sure he nodded obediently while Dad expressed his disdain for the bloody American imperialists and his sympathy for the communists in Vietnam.

As they approached the hunting grounds Randy got dizzy with trepidation. He hoped once he fired his first shot he would lose his fear, his virginity. The bullet would crack through the muddle in his mind and body, set him on the path to manhood, make him tough enough to pass muster with Dad.

The first few hours were mostly foggy boredom with much attention going to marking a path so they wouldn't get lost. Dad was ready for a bit of sustenance but Randy had forgotten to bring the sandwiches. Randy offered to run back to the car but Dad told him to just stay put while he went. They'd pretty much walked in a circle so he'd be back soon.

Randy sat leaning against a stump. Apart from forgetting the sandwiches, things weren't going too badly. In a couple hours, the light would be gone so maybe he wouldn't have to be initiated today. He was getting cold, his stomach rumbled. He rolled a cigarette, put it to his mouth. He didn't light it but let it hang off his lips the way Dad did when he was working or reading. The patter of rain filled the silence and Randy smiled thinking Dad would probably call it quits. They could go have soup at the Jolly Roger Inn and look down at the hidden cove where pirates used to take shelter after ambushing ships. Dad didn't have any romantic notions about pirates; they were like the beachcombers who broke booms and scavenged the spoils of working men like him, but he enjoyed drinking at the Jolly Roger.

Just when his anxiety about firing a rifle had evaporated, Randy saw a deer. It was on a hill maybe forty feet away, listening for anything that might be a threat. Randy got to his feet and the deer jerked its head in his direction. It was a clear shot, no obstructions. This was it, he had to do something, the gun was in his hands, it was loaded. He lifted the butt to his shoulder, undid the safety, aimed and fired. The deer barely flinched, didn't even buckle, just ran, straight toward Randy. It came so close Randy could hear the sound of its hooves hitting the earth. Then he saw the hole ripped through its stomach. He saw its innocent eyes stunned by the assault, frantic to get home, to be safe. It came so close Randy could smell the blood oozing from deep within—so close he could feel the frantic pounding of its heart. He had to stop it. He had to help it. He followed it into the thick woods, through the tangled brush, up the spongy hill. "Hey!" he called. "I'm sorry, I'm sorry, I'm sorry." He propelled himself through the blur of green wetness, not feeling the blackberry bushes scratching his face or the devil's claw tearing at his arms. "I'm sorry!" he cried out. He didn't hear the shout to stop until Dad was gripping him by the scruff of his neck.

"You fool, I told you to never chase a deer." Dad pushed him to the ground, where Randy hugged his knees and wept.

They searched until dark but never found the wounded animal. The meat was spoiled anyway.

We moved into a new house but didn't have to change schools. Now it was just a longer walk. Halfway up School Hill, Randy would veer into the woods where we used to have our fort and disappear for the day. The teachers stopped asking where he was. He was now officially expelled. Mom had never had discipline problems with us. We weren't interested in creating any more instability in our lives. But Randy was getting sour on everything.

He made friends with a spindly little hustler named Mickey, who was only fourteen but had the demeanor of a seasoned criminal. He was stunted, probably from smoking, a child gone hard. Mom said Mickey was a predator and begged Randy to stay away from him, but she had no control. He started sneaking out at night to hang with Mickey.

One night, I saw them squatting on the delivery ramp at Ken's Market with plastic bags up to their faces. When I asked what they were doing, Mickey passed his bag to me. There was a rag with some kind of solvent on it. "Sniff it," he said.

It felt like going backward on a swing with my head upside down, times a hundred. I knew the fumes would unleash something bad in me. "Let's go home," I said, but Randy just stuck his head back into the bag.

When I told him I was going to tell Mom, Randy looked at me with bleary eyes, his face slack and stupid, worse than Dad at his drunkest. He didn't know what I was saying. At home Dad was just leaving to pick up Mom from work.

"Randy's over beside Ken's Market doing drugs," I blurted out, then wished I hadn't. A half hour later Dad came home shoving Randy down the hall to his room.

"You're going to end up a brain-dead bum drooling into your lap down on Hastings Street," he yelled.

Bobby sat up in his bed, still asleep.

Mom shouted at Dad, "I'll deal with it!" Then Bobby started to cry.

"You're a bum," Randy said.

Dad growled and lifted his fist, ready to punch. He was never violent with us beyond a growl and that was enough to make us cower. Mom screamed at Dad to stop and shoved him out the door.

When Bobby stopped crying, I knew she was stroking his head and shushing him back to sleep. She came out and made Randy a milky cup of tea with lots of sugar and brought it in to him.

A few nights later, after everyone had gone to bed, I heard a creaking in the hallway. The closet door opened. Randy was getting a jacket, snooping in Dad's pockets for change, rifling through Mom's purse. He grabbed something from the fridge and went out the front door.

Mickey and Randy hatched a scheme to hitchhike across the country. Mickey had a dad who was incarcerated somewhere in Nova Scotia, and he convinced Randy it would be an adventure to track him down. Between the two of them, they had about six dollars. They hadn't thought about food or weather. They hadn't thought about hostile weirdos, who were less scary than the kind weirdo who would offer them a place to sleep but then try to lie down with them. They ran out of steam in Brandon, Manitoba. Randy had never been so hungry, so cold, or so far away—if he could have just scrounged enough money to catch a bus home, then he would never do something this stupid again. He didn't have a dime to call Mom collect. The cement was too cold to sit on and his legs would not support him anymore, so he squatted on a window sill. Mickey straightened a long butt he found on the sidewalk and was begging for a light. Forget about money, people wouldn't give them a light.

When the police showed up, Randy was relieved. They were in trouble but he'd rather be in a detention hall than starving in subzero streets. They were taken to a dull institution with nowhere comfortable to sit and some scary-looking characters, but the warmed-over gruel they slopped onto his plate was a welcome dinner. Randy kept his head down at the table and methodically replenished himself. Some of the guys were staring hard at him and he didn't want to engage them. He'd never been around people like this before. Mickey stared back at them defiantly. Randy decided he was not going to hang around with Mickey anymore. He couldn't wait to sleep. Soon he would be home. He was going back to school. He was going to help Mom and take his brother sledding down School Hill. He was going to ask Dad if he could help on the tugs to make some money. He wanted to buy a nice guitar. He wasn't going to smoke anymore, or ever sniff glue. He was not like Mickey.

When the call from Brandon came, Dad was in his cups and feeling righteous about tough love. If Mom had been there she would have made sure Randy got home right away.

Dad told the police, "Keep him for a while, teach him a lesson."

Several weeks later Randy came back. His eyes seemed to be in a permanent wince. His mouth was turned down. He sat with his back unnaturally straight reading the Bible and smoking so much his fingertips were burnt orange. He wouldn't talk to me. He started cutting long gashes across his arms, trying to bleed the voices out. He seared his limbs with cigarettes to burn the voices out. He stomped around to curse and throw them out. Mom took him to see a psychologist, and that's when he grabbed the glass ashtray and tried to cut his throat and the doctor asked Mom what she'd done to him.

While Mom and Dad were working and us kids were at school, Randy took one of Dad's rifles and shot through his hand.

Dad spiked Randy's coffee with a bunch of downers and told him we were going to get his hand fixed. But we took him to Essendale, a mental institution.

On the way to the ferry we passed some hippie girls hitchhiking with their dog and Dad actually slowed down to stop and pick them up. Mom snapped, "Don't you dare."

On the ferry Mom stayed below in the car with Randy while Dad and I went upstairs to the cafeteria. The hippie girls showed up and Dad, eager to be distracted from the gloomy silence between us, welcomed them to sit at our table. He wasn't overly cheerful but he was disassociated from the purpose of the day. When the girls, who were noticeably unshaven, complained how the crew wouldn't let them bring their dog upstairs, Dad quipped, "Well at least you got away with those squirrels under your armpits."

Mom examined Randy's face while he slept. She hadn't been able to really look at him for a long time, he'd become so private and complicated. Whenever she got close, he'd shut her out. His cheeks weren't plump and smooth anymore, they were hollowed out and the little tufts of hair trying to sprout caused patches of tiny bloodless pimples. He had no color in his skin. It seemed to have just happened, this shift. He wasn't a boy anymore but he wasn't a man. She didn't like the way his hair stuck to his forehead, he had such a fine forehead. She pushed the hair back and he reflexively raised a hand to swat her away. His eyes rolled open and found her. "Hi, Mom," he slurred. "Are we . . ." he nodded off. Mom moved closer and hugged his arm, careful to avoid his injured hand. She didn't want to send him to a hospital. If she thought she could have made him better she would have stayed beside him forever, but she couldn't. "You're going to get better," she whispered. "They're going to make you better." We finished the long tranquil drive listening to classical music on Dad's radio.

Essendale was appropriately gothic, set into the side of a mountain under thick clouds surrounded by a tall brick wall. All the windows had bars over them.

An East Indian doctor unwrapped the bandage on Randy's hand and gently touched around the wound, asking how it felt.

"Very good. Not very good," Randy said, imitating his Indian accent.

Two big male nurses appeared and Randy's chemical tranquility dissipated. He turned to Mom. Her eyes were watering and red from no sleep. Her shapeless black coat made her look more pale than she was. The sleeves drooped and her skinny arms poked out like sticks. The doctor held Randy's hand. It didn't look like a hand; it didn't look like anything I could identify. The center was a black crater that had erupted so much blood all the color was gone except for traces of green where his knuckles would be if there wasn't so much swelling.

The door from where the nurses appeared had a glass window with wire mesh that led to another door, a bolted door—a big impervious blank. The jolt of betrayal brought feeling to Randy's eyes, made greener by a flush coming to his cheeks. His jaw and mouth were open, a child asking, "Why?" Dad's mouth was set in a hard frown, dry eyes fixed on the ground, braced for the inevitable, but Mom's eyes were all water mixed with the blood of birth and the memory of innocent love, thinking she would always protect her little boy, wishing she could keep him from becoming a part of all the sickness behind that door.

Randy sprang to his feet and ran to the exit. The nurses pounced on him and muscled him back toward the passage. He cracked the wire-meshed window with his good fist and screamed out "Mom!" before the blank door bolted shut, sealing him in with the voices that I'll always believe were mine.

Mom looks at the ringing phone as if it were a growling dog. It's morning, I've been up all night.

"Is that Barbara?" the beatnik mumble of Dad's hipster friend, Pete the Poet, greets me.

"Ya."

"It's a drag, such a drag."

I can barely understand his slurred words. He's not high, it's just the way he talks. He stretches out vowels and interjects long growly *hmms*, like he's having a million thoughts at once, but when he reads his poetry he's clear. I used to think he was the oddest person I'd met. He'd stand staring at the floor with his mouth open, his face twisting with thoughts, then he'd raise his finger about to speak and say nothing. He lived with his tiny mother, whom I'd see walking, her arms weighted to the ground with heavy grocery bags that she was carrying home to feed him and his brother. She was a famous elocutionist in England who wrote many novels, was married four times, widowed twice, beaten, abandoned, and was still standing, albeit a little hunched. Pete was once a logger and writes poems about being a logger. He would sit for hours with Dad at the beer parlor to swap tales of the woods.

In my book Pete had always been just another drinker. It wasn't until I came to visit him at The Shack, a converted garage on his mother's property, that I realized he was a poet. There was an Underwood typewriter on a coffee table cluttered with pages in front of his bed, which had a big indentation where he sat writing every conscious hour he wasn't drinking. The walls were covered with shelves sagging from stacks of books and manuscripts. Pete's a nut for fantasy comic books, loves all the Beat poets, and is a big fan of John

Wayne. When I was thirteen, he gave me *Desolation Angels* and *On the Road* and asked me if I'd marry him.

"Hey, I'm ahhhhhhh . . . there's an anthology of my poetry with Al Purdy. . . . Ya, it just got published . . . Ya," he said.

After reading everything Pete loaded me up with, I started to appreciate the poetry of bleak places. His poems were harsh and melancholic, but they also elevated Dad's world. They gave a mythological dimension to what he did. He became heroic. One of Pete's poems, "Skookumchuck," grabbed me because I have a picture of Dad hanging his jeans on a clothesline in front of the Skookumchuck in the Sechelt Inlet, where he was clear-cutting a hillside.

> The ruined watersheds and wrung slopes
> Where new roads snake past the snowline
> And black amputated claws
> Of charred stumps
> Grip dirt in the scar country.

Skookumchuck is a Chinook Indian word that means "strong water" and refers to what happens with the constant tidal changes passing through a very small inlet—swift rapids, whirlpools, and eddies. Everything about logging was perilous. I was grateful that somebody who really knew the life could write about it. Pete's friend, Milton Acorn, another great Canadian poet, called Pete the Poet Laureate of the West Coast Working Class.

"You're gonna be okay," he tells me. "You and me, we're autodidacts, self-taught . . . we're artists. Randy had some heavy karma he just couldn't work through, that's just the way it goes."

"How many programs should I get printed up?" I ask Mom. My eyes are bleary from writing curlicues all night.

"Mary Dory's coming," she says. Mary is a big-boned raucous woman who owns a horse ranch on the peninsula. Her husband was driving drunk and got decapitated when his pick-up truck went off the road last year. I remember her saying, "He died with a smile on his face."

"There are six of us, plus Uncle Bill, Red, and Colleen," she adds. "And Misty."

"Should I try to get in touch with Dana?"

"No, Dana doesn't want to see us."

I call some of Dad's other friends, another poet and inventor who I like because he's a teetotaler, and painter who I suspect wound up with Granddad's art supplies. All Dad's friends are interesting. I think Marlene has some friends coming. Bobby and Kate probably won't invite their schoolmates.

Any friends Randy had have disappeared—in institutions, lost in the streets, hitchhiking on highways, or unidentified in morgues.

Mom won't invite anyone. People like Mom. They always have something nice to say about her—she's so pretty, she's so sweet, she's cool, she's kind—but she doesn't have friends.

Sky Falling

One day Mom got out of bed after another night of no sleep, believing that she had to stop the morning ferry. Convinced her car was wired to explode, she started running the three miles to the terminal, sticking her thumb out when cars passed. Soon enough, her boss pulled over.

"Car trouble, Simone?" he asked.

Simone couldn't be sure he wasn't one of the conspirators, but she didn't want to set off any alarms, so she opened the door and calmly sat down.

"Where're ya going, Sim?" Mr. Big tested her.

Did he know that she knew? "Where are you going?" she countered, looking straight into his eyes.

"Well, I'm going to work"

"So am I."

"Really?" Now he was suspicious. "I thought you were working afternoons."

Electrodes started pulsing in Simone's brassiere. They were tracking her. Big was definitely in on it. Wiggling her arms out of the straps, she deftly pulled off the wired bra and threw it out the window. Big's mouth dropped.

"I switched shifts with Heather," she said.

"Alright," he nodded carefully, "let's go to work."

Let's go to work indeed, she thought. What kind of work were these maniacs up to? What's the scheme? Everyone gets blown up? They come back when the dust settles and take all the timber? Where are their children? In that hidden bomb shelter they built for themselves and their families, hoarding all the canned goods and toilet paper from Fletcher's Market?

"Is there something wrong, Simone?" He was twitching. There was no turning back now, she had to stop the morning ferry. Randy was right. No one believed him but he had been right all along, they were listening to everything. That's why they had to get rid of Randy, because he was onto them. But she was going to stop the ferry and bring Randy home, then everybody would know he had been right.

"Of course there's something wrong," she snarled at him.

He was approaching his designated parking spot. Simone saw her route and jumped out of the car as he started to slow down. She quickly whisked through the employee gate.

"Hi, Simone!" the guard called out after her.

"Hi!" she shouted as she burst into a full sprint toward the loudspeaker control booth. People were returning to their cars in anticipation of the next boarding announcement. She was going to make it. She was going to save the whole peninsula.

Tom was opening the door to the booth. Tom liked her. He asked her out on a secret date once because he knew she was unhappily married, not even married. He wasn't part of the conspiracy, he was too young, too good.

"Can I come in?" she said, trying to catch her breath and seem calm.

"It's pretty small in here, Sim, but okay." He was amused. "What's going on?"

"I lost my purse . . . somewhere . . . I wanted to ask if anyone's seen it."

"Sure, what's it look like?" Tom switched on the P.A., ready to make an announcement.

Mr. Big and two security guys were rushing toward the booth. Simone grabbed the microphone. "Don't get on the ferry!" She yelled. "This is an emergency, do not start your cars!"

Mom was hauled away in a straitjacket and got put on disability for a while. She needed a little hiatus to get over her embarrassment and to catch up on sleep.

I decided it was time to make some cash, beyond babysitting. It was summertime and I made my way to the strawberry fields of Aldergrove. Picking berries is back-breaking work. You alternate between squatting, kneeling, and bending over. The foreman walked up and down the rows making sure we weren't slacking off. All that was missing was his whip. After eight hours of toil, I would be hallucinating strawberries. I'd be walking to the bathroom and my body would bend down to pick an imaginary red thing in the dirt. I dreamt about giant strawberries.

At night, the doors to our bunks were bolted from the outside. Why, I don't know—to keep us from stealing strawberries or running away? Fortunately my bunkmates were two sisters who were full of fun and chomping for adventure.

One night there was a folk festival happening down the road and we were determined to go. I hid outside the cabin before our door was locked and opened it after the foreman left. We flew the coop down to a wonderland of music. Bearded men and girls dressed like fairies danced around booths filled with handmade candles and tie-dye shirts. There was a strong smell of marijuana mixed with unfamiliar spices and the air was charged with sex. I wandered into a barn and sat on a hay bale beside a young woman with long silky blond hair.

Someone said, "Sing something, Joni."

The blond woman picked up her guitar and started singing, "Rows and flows of angel hair, and ice cream castles in the air."

I'd never heard a voice like that. I'd never heard guitar playing like that. I was stunned. It was the most magical music moment of my life. Afterward, an elegant hippie with a goatee wrapped his arm around her and ushered her out of the barn, leaving a handful of privileged listeners with gaping mouths.

Later, I heard that same psychedelic angel voice emanating from the turret of a wooden silo that had been decorated to look like a tower from a medieval castle. There was a male voice singing harmony and a blend of guitars. Someone said it was Graham Nash up there with her. I was inspired and shut down at the same time, I guess that's what envy is. The girls and I crawled back to our hovel for a few hours sleep before we busted our bodies another day, while the golden songstress and her lover kept singing the night away in their enchanted tower.

My ninth-grade English teacher believed I had a good voice. When I was in his class, he had me sing "Barbara Allen" and "House of the Rising Sun" to illustrate different types of meters in songs. He paid for me to take singing lessons with Mrs. Vernon, whose daughter was a professional opera singer. On Saturday mornings, I'd climb across Gospel Rock to her home overlooking the harbor and sing "Elijah! Get thee hence Elijah!" with a hooty voice that was not cool or natural. She drilled scales and intervals into my head and tried to make me breathe correctly.

Then Mr. Pete set up an audition for me at the CBC. Mrs. Vernon wanted me to sing Mendelssohn but I opted for Hank Williams.

On the ferry over to Vancouver, I ran into a cab driver named Michael, a handsome man who used to give me rides up School Hill. I was planning to stay overnight at the Y because my audition was early in the morning. I had my bus route all mapped out, but he drove me into Vancouver and invited me to stay with his friends. It seemed like a good offer—I was nervous about being in the city by myself for the first time, not to mention the terror I was feeling about auditioning. Michael was a charming guy, I liked the way he dressed.

His friends, a tall skinny blond woman and her equally skinny husband, gave us the remains of their Chinese food and I did a test run of "I'm so Lonesome I could Cry" to their cheers and applause. I bedded down on a mat in their backroom with visions of making a record and singing for a big audience swirling me into twilight.

Through the night I heard more people arriving at the apartment, their voices barely audible under a thick blanket of jazz music on the hi-fi. Just when I was starting to dream, I heard a shout. "Michael! Michael! Wake up! Shit. Shit. Shit. He's fucking OD'ed! Goddamnit!" My heart started racing. I got up. In truth, I was less concerned about Michael than I was about my guitar, which I found precariously propped in the hallway. Through a closed door I heard slapping sounds. "Come on man!" they kept saying. "Wake up!" Then there was a laugh of relief. "Shit man, you gave us a scare."

I went back to bed with my guitar and purse safe under the covers with me. I wasn't planning to sleep but my eyes closed and suddenly the sun was pounding through the window. Michael was passed out on top of the covers beside me. My guitar and purse were intact. I got dressed and washed my face. All seemed okay, except I couldn't find one of my shoes. I scoured the room and the apartment, probably turning over remnants of heroin paraphernalia, not that I would have known what it looked like. My shoe was nowhere. I had to leave, my appointment was in ten minutes. I wondered if I should wear one shoe. In a hall closet, there were some sandals twice my size, but I couldn't keep them on my feet even if I wanted to. I opened a bedroom door to find the blond woman and man lying face up on their bed like corpses, naked. I felt like I'd go to hell if I stayed another minute.

I ran barefoot to the CBC and got there on time, flushed and breathless. It wasn't that cold, the dirt on the sidewalk bothered me more. Everyone pretended not to notice my bare feet, maybe that's what they were expecting, some wild child down from the boondocks. I was ushered into a little glassed-in booth with a microphone hanging down from above. A man gave me headphones to put on and a voice came through asking to get a level. I took so many deep breaths to calm myself that I got dizzy. Then my foot doubled up on itself. I pressed my toes into the floor, trying to push the cramp away.

"Any time you're ready," the voice said.

My fingers were shaking too badly to fingerpick, so I strummed—"You hear the lonesome Whippoorwill, he sounds too blue to fly."

I didn't recognize the voice coming into my headphones. I wasn't even close to being on pitch. The engineer encouraged me to try again, but every time I opened my mouth, I croaked. The more I tried the worse it sounded.

I cowered all the way home. I quit singing lessons and avoided Mr. Pete at every turn.

I decided I had to get a real job. Making money was the only opportunity I saw. Mom and Dad didn't instill a belief that we could do better than they did. I never considered that someone like me could go to university. The way to get ahead was to get to work.

Brian's Drive-In was the only hangout on the peninsula. It stayed open later than any other business and was directly across from the high school.

I was fifteen but told Brian I was sixteen and he hired me on the spot.

I worked from four o'clock until midnight, shutting the drive-in down, sometimes getting home at two in the morning, then I'd put in a full day at school.

My eyes had violet circles under them, my skin got all pimply from hormone shifts and greasy french-fry shifts. The veins in my legs started to bulge. I have no pictures from that time, just the memory of feeling like I was nothing but my flaws. The drive-in was drudge work, tedious and dull, except when someone special like RZ dropped in.

He was my first teenage crush. He had black hair, black eyes, tight black pants, black boots like The Beatles, and a black motorcycle jacket. I'd always take his order, too shy to start a conversation, but one night he asked me if I'd like to go to a party. Lucky me. I got off work early, ran home, and put on the only pretty dress I had, a full-length empire-waisted salmon-colored polyester bridesmaid's dress that I'd made for the shotgun wedding of my friend Lynn, who once boasted she'd had sex with RZ.

At the party, RZ taught me Muddy Water's "Freight Train" on guitar, amidst a motorcycle gang drinking heavily and smashing beer bottles on the kitchen floor. He drove me in a big-finned greaser car to his dad's house in Port Melon. His father was head foreman at the pulp mill there. The sulfur in the air was sickening.

We sat on the couch while he drank more beer and mumbled through "Mr. Tambourine Man" on an out-of-tune guitar. His German shepherd Lobo growled every time I shifted. It was like Dad was sitting there. I was ready to go home but instead I ended up in his bedroom, with him trying to be amorous. I wanted the deed to be over but it never happened. He was so drunk he kept falling off the bed. My crush and the polyester dress got mangled together. And after his last fall, RZ never got up. While he snored on the floor, I crept to the bathroom and was cornered by Lobo. If I even looked at the room where RZ was sleeping, Lobo would bear his teeth. Finally, I heard wheels on gravel, his dad's night shift was over. Lobo ran to the front door and I escaped out the back. I sat in RZ's car until hours later when he emerged, hungover and very unappealing.

He dropped me at the apartments in the gloomy dawn and the last thing he said was, "Keep singing, Barb."

That incident created a queasiness in me toward sex, which was reinforced by my guidance teacher, a British Army Sergeant–type with short, steely gray hair. She lived with another woman, and I recall talk of her being a lesbian, which seemed a peaceful alternative to putting up with a man. In her class, she showed us sex education films that were so dull it was a relief to giggle over the illustration of a penis. She got a big laugh when she told us, with unmasked disdain, that men just do their business then roll over and go to sleep.

Mom and I were mutually uncomfortable over body issues. I couldn't talk to her about what to do with my blossoming bosom. I would clutch my hands at my neck and make a cross of my arms to shield my breasts, keeping away the evil eye, as well as supporting them. I eventually stole a brassiere from the women's wear store at the strip mall beside school. It was too big but it was better than bare nipples poking out.

Ditto with sanitary napkins. I was caught stealing at Ken's Market by Ken, whose kids I used to babysit. When he saw what I had under my coat he just turned away and told me not to do it again. Mom didn't like her story, so she never told us anything. We were like wild animals with the wrong set of instincts for our environment.

My boss Brian won a mandocello in a poker game. I'd never seen or heard an instrument like it, tear-shaped and with such a bright tone, like a mandolin but it had a flat back and was deep and resonant like a guitar. He said I could have it in exchange for making seat covers and curtains for the drive-in. I put my Home-Ec training to use, taking detailed measurements of the seats and creating a pattern, then Brian gave me a hundred bucks for fabric. I caught the ferry over to Vancouver, this time avoiding any familiar faces.

I knew the Army and Navy Store on Hastings Street because it was down the street from the Patricia Hotel, where Dad picked up logging work and got sloshed. It was a big, badly lit place brimming with cheap merchandise. I bought several yards of fabric and got out of there quickly because the store lights gave me a headache.

I had hours to kill before the bus back to the ferry, so I started to wander and saw that *The Prime of Miss Jean Brodie* was playing at a cinema in a half-hour. I sat down at the counter of a diner and ordered coffee. I should have had something to eat, but then I wouldn't have had enough money for the movie. I pulled out a cigarette I'd stolen from Dad and was searching for a light. A man sat beside me and held up a match. He said his name was Sam. He was Greek.

I told him I was going to see the movie and he asked if he could come with me. I said okay, though I really didn't want him to. He was repulsive. He was very short and you could barely see his eyes for his overgrown eyebrows. He had thick hair on the back of his hands. I felt sorry for him. As we walked to the cinema, I kept pulling down my little plaid miniskirt, regretting that I'd made it so short.

I told him I had a boyfriend, which wasn't true, but I thought he might get the hint and stop touching my back.

I told him he didn't have to pay for my ticket but he did.

Someday I'll savor watching *The Prime of Miss Jean Brodie* without a stranger staring at me in the dark and breathing close to me.

I told him I had to catch the bus. He asked me to stop at his hotel because he had a present for my boyfriend.

This will be incomprehensible to anyone who grew up thinking they had a right to say what they did and didn't want. I told him, "Okay."

He was such an ugly man, like a little beast that God forgot. I thought I was being kind, though I gritted my teeth when he kept prodding me up the hotel stairs. How stupid was I to think that my kindness would protect me?

I told him I didn't want anything to drink. And when I saw it was a ring he wanted to give my fictional boyfriend, something he might have cut off someone's finger for, I started to feel sick. I told him I had to go. He started putting money in the bag with all the fabric. He said something that indicated he wanted sex. I stood up and grabbed my stuff and threw all the money on the floor. "I have to go," I said, as I rushed to the door.

But he grabbed my wrist and told me not to get hysterical or he'd hurt me. I should have fought, should have hit him and run out the door. But I felt strangely paralyzed. Like I deserved to be punished because I was stupid enough to walk into this situation. I took the bottle of rye whiskey. I hated alcohol, it poisoned everything, but I drank the entire pint. I tried to hold my knees together but the dizziness set in. The ceiling was a swirling *me me me*, there was a gas pedal in my stomach, and the room smelled like cats.

When my guts started to spill up, the beast dragged me out to the bathroom in the hallway. He stood in the hall and in a lucid moment I bolted the door. I broke the window with a tin of comet cleanser, scraped through the opening, and fell from the fire escape into the alley. My skirt was pushed up to my waist, there was blood on my legs. I ran until I saw people. I asked where the bus depot was. I staggered in circles and then I was there. I had no purse. I begged for money. And then I was on the ferry, so I must have caught the bus. I don't know how many times I threw up. Through dizzy cafeteria lights, I searched for Mom. She wasn't on the cash register or taking orders or flipping burgers. I would have eaten one of those noxious burgers, just to be fed by her, but she wasn't working. I think I passed out somewhere. One of the ship's crew dropped me in front of our apartment building.

The next morning I woke up poisoned. When I tried to stand pain shot through my body. My ankle was huge and purple.

Mom drove me to the medical clinic on her way to work. She was late and couldn't stay. I told her I tripped on the sidewalk in the city. She didn't ask any questions, I think maybe she thought I had got into some trouble and didn't want to know.

The doctor looked at my ankle and said I'd have to get x-rays at the hospital, but he was pretty sure it was dislocated, if not broken. I thought of telling him what had happened, but he would just think I was stupid.

Being on crutches brought some sympathy. I ended up in a cast. No shame in a broken ankle. Painkillers hit the spot like ice cream when I had the measles, I had no appetite for anything else. My boss gave me the Mandocello anyway, whether he bought my story of being robbed or not.

Rape was dramatic, it was primary colors, red and blue, blood and bruise make purple. I wore them inside.

On account of that episode, I had a flashback of sorts, a hazy memory started to come into focus of something unpleasant happening to me in Mr. Russell's house back in Bear Creek when I was five years old. I saw his wife sitting in her wheelchair in the kitchen, her sightless eyes staring in the direction of a radio on the counter. Her face had given up, her shoulders sagged into her sagging dress. The CBC News was mutilated by static. I'm lying on my stomach on a bed looking through a crack in the door. She can't see me but I know she knows I'm there. It's a small bed. Is it for a child? Mr. Russell is behind me and his hand is covering my mouth. His fingers gouge into my cheeks and all I can do is breathe through my nose. His hand smells like tobacco smoke and sour milk. I feel an awful pressure where I'm not supposed to. I try to count the spokes on the wheelchair but keep losing my place and start over.

Over the years Dad would sometimes joke about Old Ed

Russell. "Old Ed on the playground with his toys." "Old Ed didn't have all his oars in the water but he was a mechanical whiz."

One morning, I was sneaking Kahlua in my coffee before I went to school. Dad came in cursing because the car had broken down and he was late for work.

"I wish Old Ed were around, he'd have it running in a minute."

"If Old Ed were here, I'd stab him in the heart," I said.

That was all I ever revealed to Dad.

I was tired all the time. Mom wanted me to come visit Randy at Essendale with her, but I figured we would just make each other feel worse.

Later that year, I was still frying up pimplemakers and future heart disease. After a full day of not learning at school—but alert on account of the dexedrine pills I'd been stealing from Dad's top drawer—a handsome guy with a fun smile under a big moustache switched on some unfamiliar light in me. Ben was a lying drug dealer, but I didn't know that. He leaned over the counter to kiss me and the rancid grease coating my face was so much lubricant.

We hit a deer driving through a blizzard up to his cabin. He slung it in the back of his pick-up truck, wondering what kind of psychedelics the commune up the inlet would give him in trade. The rigid carcass made me shudder. I only kissed Ben because I was cold. I smoked pot and grew fearful about sneaking in late, then Dad waking up to smell guilt on me. I imagined we were stranded, that the whole peninsula was buried. I would never find my way back home.

In a short time, I was living with Ben on Sammy's ranch. Sammy was a draft-dodging hippie from Northern California, floating on a trust fund with his wife, Rosie, a raven-haired stoner who tortured Sammy with put-downs and infidelities.

I spent my free hours playing guitar with Sammy.

Sometimes I hitchhiked to school, sometimes I caught a bus. Everyone was too hungover to drive me in the morning. After school, I walked across the street and put in eight hours, then Sammy usually picked me up.

I finally made the seat-covers for Brian with material we bought locally. Ben gave me speed so I could keep working. Pot brought me right to the edge and beyond—I had to lie on my back under chairs holding onto their wooden legs to stop free-falling into paranoia. I tried drinking but it made me sick before it made me better. Speed worked. It was a way to get through the day, it wasn't for entertainment.

I was depleted. I missed Randy, but that person didn't exist anymore. I didn't want to go home. I couldn't look after anyone and no one could look after me.

It was Thanksgiving, no school. I said I'd work but as the hour approached, I decided I would rather die. I found a stash of horse tranquilizers Ben had. I think half a pill could put down a horse. I crushed four of them in a glass of orange juice and sat sipping as I wrote my suicide note.

"Tell Brian I won't be in for work today, Barbara."

I walked down the driveway already feeling better because I wasn't going to work. Sammy and Ben were coming from the stable.

"Pick you up at midnight?" Sammy said.

"Sure."

And then they each grabbed an arm and flipped me over, so smoothly that it seemed choreographed. I was standing on my feet and they were walking into the house saying, "Goodbye."

"Goodbye."

And I disappeared into the woods.

It was mid-autumn, Indian summer. The evergreens were lightly spaced with red and gold deciduous trees. I heard Sammy and Brian calling for me, confused by my note. They must have seen me go into the woods instead of toward the bus stop. I climbed high up a maple tree and shimmied out on a long branch. The ocean below glimmered in the low light of the sun. I just wanted to go down to the beach, to let the salt air fill my lungs, to feel the smooth pebbles under my bare feet, to climb over the mossy cliffs, to walk across the logs that bridged the crevices, to touch the flesh of arbutus trees, their peeling red bark. Why didn't I just call in sick? Why let a job ruin my life? Then I fell.

I was suspended between a sea breeze and the breath of conifers exhaling in unison, floating within a collision of currents.

Somewhere a mother was licking clean her knock-kneed fawn and restless swallows were keeping vigil over fragile eggs, eggs nestled in a bed of scrounged scraps held together by their mother's spit and shit. The disappearing ocean glistened silver. The twisted red trunks of arbutus trees stood out like a Chinese brush painting on the silk horizon, their graceful foliage masking the strain of desperate roots gripping granite, clinging to unyielding cliffs. I was weightless. Insignificant.

Crows laughed from a ringside perch unseen. Large downy branches did not reach out to save me. With the thud of earth, my body returned, face down, heavy as a hundred dead cows.

A punishing ache radiated to every part of me. My lungs begged for breath, my mouth snapped, air rushed in and with it the taste of decomposing leaves, layers and layers of fallen things rotted and part of the ground. My vision divided into an array of universes—in each, hundreds of ants were hauling bits of leaf. Some eyed my face. One stepped forward and stole a crumb of snot from my nose. I snorted, but the little workers would not stop, they swarmed. I couldn't locate my hands to swat them away. I couldn't feel where my neck joined my torso. My face was planted in mulch. This was the end of me. I would be recycled by industrious ants. Never again would I serve french fries and dead meat to pus-faced adolescents, or fight off the boozy passes of tattooed longshoremen, or think about the Greek beast's hands. I would never have to bear another greasy night of dimwitted chatter. I'd never have to look at the dead-end of my life in the pulp-mill worker's eyes. I saw worms feasting on my intestines, wondered what scavenger would carry away my heart. I hoped I was dead before the crows ate my eyes.

My screen went dim, ants scoured my face, all systems down, no thoughts, just dirt in the ground.

It might have ended then if I hadn't tried to swallow one last time. My mouth was dry as cured wood, unable to produce a spittle of moisture. I wanted to fade, not suffocate. My hands and knees found ground. Through devils claws and thorny teeth I crawled toward the gurgle of Robert's Creek.

Mom was in a cloud hovering over me with a woeful look on her face and I thought I might be dead, but then she said, "How ya feelin', Barb?" and I knew no one would call me Barb in the afterlife.

I was in the hospital. The horse tranquilizers were a catastrophe. If you can't kill yourself completely, don't bother trying. Now I was hooked up to monitors and IVs were rehydrating me. They fed me charcoal tablets, purged my bowels, detoxified my liver. They woke me up every hour to walk me. Oxygenate me.

A family had fished me out of their backyard creek in time to save me from drowning, but it was too late to pump my stomach. My swan dive from the maple tree gave me a few dislocated ribs and a wrenched neck, and I was gouged from crawling through the blackberry bushes, but that was all minor compared to the pill damage. By day I dozed and dreamed but, at night, when the haze burned off, I was bug-eyed with bleak thoughts. I lost my job at the drive-in. Not because of the suicide attempt, but because my boss found out I was only fifteen when I started working for him.

Sammy showed up to tell me the RCMP had come by his ranch. I wondered if Dad tipped them off. Dad saw no hypocrisy in condemning my Crow Road digs as a nest for low-life druggies. Which was true, but it was unfair that Sammy came under scrutiny for what I did. Luckily no one got busted but Sammy thought it would be uncool for me to come back. Ben didn't show. I'm sure he was afraid of a run in with Dad.

The woman in the bed next to me was from California. She was on vacation and something went wrong with her heart. She had a confidence I associated with America and California in particular. I told her I tried to kill myself and she gave me a mother's hug like I'd never had.

"Don't you ever do that again," she said. "Look at you. You're a beautiful young girl with so much to look forward to."

Her son was a doctor. I didn't tell him about the rape but we talked about the voices. He said things like that might occur when another family member was mentally ill. I told him about my brother and he talked about how tragic mental illness was. He told me my empathy was a gift with a big price. He made me feel like I was normal and at the same time exceptional.

Then they flew home to the sun and I was left in the wet sulk of Gibson's Landing in November. During one of my sleep spells, *The French Lieutenant's Woman* appeared beside me. The nurse said a man with black hair and a tattoo on his arm left it. Dad believed reading brought salvation to any situation. For the next few days, I inhabited the life of a poor governess, superior to her circumstances, who portrayed herself as a fallen woman, cultivating an air of mystery rather than being overlooked for her lowly status—defined by spirit not birthright. I was oblivious to day or night, bad food soaked in hospital smells, enemas, needles, oxygen walks. I just kept reading.

I couldn't rouse myself to go back to school. Part of me wished I could just be a high school student again, smoking in the girl's

bathroom and cramming for tests, but it seemed so unimport-
ant. No one ever told me an education mattered. The school had
burned down while I was in the hospital and I took it as a sign.

I didn't have to help around the house. On top of my damaged organs and wrenched bones, they discovered I had a
heart murmur which gave me license to feel even more sorry
for myself. Ben came to our house and sat crying on the back
steps. He was shooting heroin by then. Whatever tenderness
I felt for him got knocked out of me when I fell from the
tree. Dad would've kicked him down the stairs, but he was
so pathetic, sniveling like a baby, that Dad just told him to
get along and not come back. He died that week, some say
mysteriously. He burned a lot of people, but I'm sure it was
just a plain-old overdose. Sammy came by to tell me that Ben's
friends would meet in the Peninsula Hotel parking lot, then
go toss his ashes at Gospel Rock. He asked me if I would sing.
Not a chance. I suggested they toss his ashes in the parking lot.

Mom brought leftover hamburgers from work one day, but I
couldn't bear the idea of eating meat. I wanted fresh fruit, not a
tired apple from Fletcher's Market. I wanted a sweet orange from
California, picked right off the tree. I wanted to sit on Mom's
lap while she brushed my hair and took all the tangles away. I
wanted to tell her what the Greek man did to me. I wanted her
to kiss my forehead and cradle me. But I didn't know how to tell
her. I lay on my cot in the basement of our twenty-seventh house
watching the legs of people going to and from the post office. I
breathed as little air as possible. Legs scurried, met other legs,
waddled, dawdled, and drove away. Night came and I was still
breathing. I stayed in bed for months.

Suddenly Last Summer

My tenth-grade English teacher was standing in front of my cot. I didn't care enough to be embarrassed. Mr. Burnside bugged me because he used to always put his hand on my thigh, but I liked the way he talked. He had a thick Scottish accent like Miss Jean Brodie.

"You're looking like the poor Lady of the Camellias dying of consumption," he said. I didn't know what he was talking about. He was kind of an asshole but he was interesting.

"Are you familiar with Tennessee Williams?" He knew I wasn't.

Mr. Burnside had started a theater company with Eileen Glassford, an older woman who was very involved with empowering Native kids. They wanted me to play the role of Catherine in *Suddenly Last Summer*. At school, he'd directed a little scene from *MacBeth* where I played one of the witches, but this was an extreme leap of faith. He laid the play beside me. I was trembling inside but showed nothing.

"Some people don't think you can do this, but I think you can."

After his legs cleared the basement window, I picked up the book. It was small. I turned to the first page. "New Orleans. A garden like a tropical jungle. . . . The colors of this jungle are violent . . . steaming with heat after rain. . . . massive tree-flowers that suggest organs of a body, torn out, still glistening with undried blood . . . harsh cries and sibilant hissings and thrashing sounds . . . as if it were inhabited by beasts, serpents and birds, all of a savage nature." My mind was spinning images. I thought of axes thwacking at tree trunks, the vicious teeth of chainsaws cutting into ancient giants, the amber sap bleeding through wounded bark. I thought of children smothered under mud. I thought of cats caterwauling, broken glass, hissing voices in the black of night. I started to warm up. I carried the book upstairs and made myself a cup of tea.

Catherine was shut in a mental institution, jolted with shock treatments, and made numb with medication. Everything Randy was going through. She'd been abused and misunderstood and silenced. Steam started rising all around me. Every word carried feelings to my nerve endings. Blood filled my body and my brain. Catherine needed to tell her grotesque, flesh-ripping story. I didn't know anything about acting, but I knew I could do this. I could tell my story inside someone else's story. "We're all of us children in a vast kindergarten trying to spell God's name with the wrong alphabet blocks." Tennessee Williams knew my heart!

I studied Catherine's monologues day and night until they were living inside me.

We rehearsed at the high school on weekends. It was odd being there, I felt like a pardoned criminal. I was the youngest person in the cast. There was a guy who had come back to finish high school in his late twenties, everybody else was a teacher. Mr. Burnside expressed his concern about my soft voice. He said I whispered most of the time. I knew I could be loud, I just needed permission. Whatever apprehension and awkwardness I felt, I channeled into the words I was speaking, and every nod of approval and surprised smile raised my volume. I mimicked Scarlet O'Hara's accent with a hurt in my voice like Mom's. I felt the suddenness of my sister's rages. And when my character got shot up with sodium pentothal, I invoked Randy's ramblings at the institution.

Nest Lewis, a thin and mysterious black-haired Welsh woman, who always seemed bemused by my inventiveness when she was my Home-Ec teacher, played Aunt Violet. In an understated way—"I have a lovely room in the attic that feels very empty"—she invited me to come and live at her house. Her partner was a stay-at-home writer, a big bear of a guy named Oz. When they were both gone, I babysat their little boy who loved to hear me sing. Nest said, "You're singing for your supper," and I know she said it so the room and board wouldn't feel like charity. Nest and Oz could drink wine, laugh, and disagree out loud without ever fighting. They always got up in the morning in a cheery mood.

One time Mr. Burnside was over for dinner and he was talking about how rigid the schools were in Scotland compared to Canada. "By the way," Oz said to me, "Are you ever going back to school?"

I immediately assumed I might be wearing out my welcome so I said, "No, but I'm going to start looking for a job soon."

"Hungry man, reach for the book," Mr. Burnside said in his heightened brogue, looking directly into my eyes, "it is a weapon." With his goatee and shoulder length curls, I imagined him a character from Shakespeare.

"Bertolt Brecht?" Nest asked.

"Now that's an educated woman." Mr. Burnside smiled. It took me a minute to decipher the Brecht quote. I realized it was a jab at me for being a dropout. I kept quiet as my cheeks burned, feeling like I was too ignorant to be sitting at the table. For the next few weeks, I spent most of my time in the attic, drilling my monologues.

The moment I had adjusted to the routine of rehearsing, I was standing in the wings, about to go on stage in front of an audience for the first time. The whole town was buzzing in the high school auditorium, like the ravenous street children of Cabeza de Lobo . . . my teachers, my family, friends, friends I had never had, and Granddad. I took deep breaths trying to stay in my body. Mr. Burnside shoved me on and I made a beeline to center stage. I grabbed a cigarette and looked for the wooden matches I had rehearsed with every day. The matches had been replaced by an object I didn't recognize as a lighter. I couldn't get it to work.

The nurse hustled on stage and said her first line—"What have you got in your hand?"

"Nothing, sister."

"Give me that cigarette."

I couldn't say the cigarette was already lit, so she couldn't have it. Our dialogue was derailed, and I was so panicked I spewed out my lines over hers—"Too late" . . . "Don't be such a Bully!" . . . "I'm not being Violent!"

"Alright then here take it!"

I was supposed to butt the lit cigarette into the palm of her hand, but I just threw it at her.

Then she was supposed to scream about how I'd deliberately burned her, but all she could do was shake her head in confusion.

The only way to fix this train wreck was to skip ahead to the end of the scene and yell: "Aaahhh, I'M SICK. I'M SICK!"

My tension released, our confusion cleared and the play got on course. When I reached the part where I was describing naked children on the beach chasing after me and my cousin Sebastian—they were screaming "pan, pan"—I started to go into some kind of trance. I saw the children's "frightfully thin" bodies that made them look like "a flock of plucked birds." I saw the sun "that had caught fire in the sky!" and finally I saw the flock overtake Sebastian.

How freeing it was to be in my body as someone else! Looking straight at people, into the audience, as if they were a vision of horror. I saw them cut "parts of him away with their hands or knives or maybe those jagged tin cans they made music with." I saw bits of Sebastian being stuffed "into those gobbling fierce little empty black mouths of theirs . . ." I was overwhelmed with tears.

And I was psychically spent, I could barely stand. Nest grabbed my hand. The audience was applauding. We bowed. For the first time in my life, I felt seen, even though they were seeing someone else.

We performed at the Provincial Drama Festival in Dawson Creek, the most northern city in B.C. This time I was prepared for the cigarette lighter and had more confidence. The hallucinations of the first performance were never as real, but I think my acting got better. It was summer and the sun never set. Neither did I. I saw *Waiting For Godot*, which made no sense to me, but I had a great time talking to the actors in it. They'd seen my performance and were impressed. We did theater workshops. There were all these young people with dreams of playing great roles and of studying at RADA and LAMDA. I was a greenhorn, but I belonged.

On the night of the awards, I was so far back in the theater I could barely hear. I wasn't really paying attention, just enjoying my plush velvet seat and the rich atmosphere. Suddenly Mr. Burnside, Mrs. Glassford, and Nest were shaking me, telling me to go on, to get up. I'd won! I walked forever down the aisle—the stage kept seeming farther away, people clapped and smiled, I grew smaller and smaller. The presenter, Tom Kerr, held me by my shoulders to stop me from shaking. "From the British Columbia Drama Association, to Barbara Williams, a young actress of great promise."

When I got back to Nest's place I received a letter from Mr. Kerr telling me I should develop my talent by going to theater school. He included an application to the Vancouver City College Theatre Arts program and a letter of recommendation. Unfortunately, to qualify, you had to have finished high school. There was no way I could go back to school now.

While I was moping about what to do, I went to see

Zefferelli's *Romeo and Juliet* at the local cinema. The actors, the music, the language, the setting—everything was so beautiful that I wept moon dust and rose petals. Then when the lights came up, everyone in the theater seemed dull and dreamless. I went home and filled out the application for theater school. Even though it warned you would be disqualified for false information, I said I graduated high school that year. I had to be an actress. Within a few weeks, I got an audition for the college. Mr. Burnside helped me prepare Juliet's balcony soliloquy, and I reworked the "hungry little black mouths" from *Suddenly Last Summer*.

I went to the audition with my Best Actress certificate and the letter of recommendation in hand. It was the first time I'd been to Vancouver since the rape. It was beautiful, this day. There was a bright blue sky against dark blue mountains, the shimmering ocean, grand homes with lush gardens. It wasn't the same city I knew. I did my monologues and brought myself to tears. I was so over the top they must have thought I was unstable. They chuckled amongst themselves.

Mr. Holland, the director of the program said, "So you burned your high school down did you?" He was holding a letter, "Your principal says . . ."

I blanched, certain I was about to be rejected for lying— ". . . that you graduated this year but all the records were destroyed in a fire?" Mr. Montgomery, aka "Monty" the vice principal the last time I was in school, the same man who gave me the strap, was now sticking his neck out to help me. The high school had burned down, but there had never been any record of me going beyond grade ten.

As I was going out the door, Mr. Holland said, "Work on something funny to have in your back pocket."

I hitchhiked back to the ferry and was picked up by a Swiss anthroposophist in a sports car. I had read a little bit about Rudolf Steiner so we talked about his approach to theater studies at the Gotheanum. I was reading another John Fowles book, *The Magus*, and I talked about how I would love to go to the Greek island Phraxos. I was trying to displace the negative association I had with Greece. The anthroposophist asked me if I'd like to taste real Greek feta cheese.

After my last encounter with a stranger in Vancouver, you would think I might have been wary, but the sun was shining on me, so I went to his home. He was the inventor of a gyrocopter displayed on the corner of his property. I sat on a living tree trunk in the middle of his kitchen and ate goat cheese and olives with the anthroposophist and his wife, who came from somewhere like Sri Lanka. She brought out more little curiosities to taste. We chewed on candied fennel seeds and drank sweet coffee with cardamon in it. The main character in *The Magus* follows a sign in the woods that says *salle d'attente*, waiting room. There he finds people who are expecting him. That's how I felt with this couple, they seemed to know I was coming. They were kind and encouraging, telling me what a wonderful road was ahead for me. They opened my senses with a dozen new tastes, then the anthroposophist drove me to the ferry terminal and wished me well.

On the ferry I saw some people I knew and asked for a ride home. They told me to meet them at the car when we landed. I sat down to read more of *The Magus*. The book grew

stranger. A schizophrenic woman turned out to be two people, herself and a twin, and they were playing a theater game
with this guy's mind. I was almost finished reading the book
when I heard the horn signaling our approach to land. But
it was the wrong shore. We were coming into Horseshoe
Bay—which I had just departed. Nobody was on the ferry
that I had embarked with. I started to think I had dreamed
the entire day and it was now just beginning. After getting
my bearings, I realized I had sat reading through the deaf-
ening horn blow on our approach to land, I hadn't noticed
the passengers disembark, the new passengers board, or the
crossing back.

Hope

I was accepted into theater school and The Driftwood Players raised a small bursary for me. Eileen Glassford connected me with a family to stay with in exchange for light housekeeping. The Greers were my dream family—for them life had a greater purpose than just surviving. They were political. They had a beautiful big house in an upscale neighborhood, but they lived modestly there. Mr. Greer was related to Tommy Douglas, the first leader of the New Democratic Party. He was tall, with big hands, silver hair, and blue eyes. He had a slow and graceful way of moving. When he spoke, he would look right at you and make you feel like what you had to say really mattered.

When I first arrived, Mr. Greer was in the backyard with his eight-year-old son, Alan, and eleven-year-old daughter, Beth, silk-screening posters for an NDP candidate in an upcoming election.

"Do you take an interest?" he asked me, and for him I did.

His wife, Nan, was a Scottish nurse who now taught

Sunday school. Mr. Greer described himself as agnostic, but Nan believed that some people needed a crutch, and that religion was better than most crutches.

I rode one of the Greer's spare bicycles to Vancouver City College and entered my first theater class, late, sweaty, and flushed, then proceeded to get more sweaty and flushed. Everyone was gathered in a circle in the movement room, which was a regular low-ceilinged classroom where a dance floor had been installed. Apart from being white and urban—all of them—the students were quite diverse: skinny, round, short, tall, pretty, plain, wearing everything from striped tights and neon sweaters to solid black ensembles. What they all had in common was their enthusiasm for talking about themselves.

We had to explain why we wanted to be actors. Some gushed about how they had always known they were destined for the stage and told cute anecdotes about jumping into the spotlight at weddings and funerals. Someone else fell in love with the works of Shakespeare in tenth grade. Some had been taking lessons in the performing arts since they were five. They were all ready for this moment. I wanted to run away and come back later with some clever fiction about myself, but it was suddenly my turn. I stammered, "Um . . . I don't know how to do anything else?" For the entire first month, I was constantly ill at ease.

My breakthrough came when we were given the assignment of performing something we had absolutely no ability in. We had a week to prepare and the objective was to give it your best effort. We performed in the auditorium in front of the entire school. Watching a big oafish guy in a tutu try-ing to pirouette, listening to a trumpet being tortured by an unskilled player, then to a tone-deaf twig of a girl sing "O Sole Mio" was high entertainment. I chose to improvise a stand-up comedy routine and did no preparation except to commit myself to saying or doing whatever came into my head. I walked on stage, looked at the audience, and fell to the ground as if in a faint. People laughed. I grabbed the mic and screamed: "I'm so sorry! I don't know what I'm doing up here. I'm a shy person . . ." The more I amplified my impulses, the more people laughed and it was a joy.

Cleaning house for the Greers was a cinch, just dusting, vacuuming, mopping, doing laundry, and their house never got that messy. They never made me feel subservient, but treated me as an equal. Their big dining room table was always filled with politicians, exchange students, and mis-sionaries engaged in conversation. I was shy to participate, but the Greers would always find a way to make me feel included. "Barbara's playing the Red Queen in *Alice In Wonderland* at theater school," they'd say. "You know she won an award at the B.C. drama festival?" At one dinner I was introduced to a friend of Mr. Greer's who was a mem-ber of Parliament. He suggested I apply for a job as a tour guide at the Parliament buildings on my summer break. Maybe he could help me out.

Sometimes the Greers would ask me to sing and I'd warble out a Bob Dylan or Joni Mitchell tune. To please Mr. Greer, I started learning Woody Guthrie songs. Some weekends I would perform at coffee houses. I was a nervous performer, my fingerpicking was jerky, and my singing voice has always been a little rough, but I managed to make pocket money by passing the hat.

One day Mom showed up in a new beige Datsun with a green racing stripe down the middle. She was cryptic about how she had acquired the wheels, only saying with a grin that somebody gave them to her. We were going to visit Randy.

My dread of Essendale had kept me away all year. Now there was a heavy rain and Mom was driving too fast on the highway, but she was so up I didn't want to take anything away from her. She had talked to Randy a few days before and he had seemed clear-headed. She went on about how he didn't like the medication and the shock treatments made him feel awful. It was time for him to get out of the hospital. Dad could probably get him a job on the tugs. Mom was sure he was better now.

We arrived at the gloomy gray building, entered through the heavy doors, and were led to a waiting room. As we were sitting there, a bald man with a smooth pink face sat down beside Mom and said something I couldn't understand. It became apparent he was a patient.

"We're here visiting my son," Mom said.

The bald man's inflections implied he made sense to himself, but his words were incomprehensible. I tried to discern if he had a speech impediment or if he was speaking a foreign language, but it was jabberwocky. Most odd was that Mom responded as if she understood him—"No, I live in Gibson's Landing. It's just north of Vancouver."

He directed a question to me, "Hincha dori momraths outgrabe?"

Mom raised her eyebrows like she was waiting for me to answer him.

"She lives in Vancouver," Mom said. She didn't care if there was meaning in his gibberish, she was responding to his tone.

"Ah brillag, brillag."

"Yes, it's very nice."

In most conversations, Mom will smile politely and tap her foot, always trying to escape. In this back and forth she seemed comfortable, almost chatty. "The seawall around Stanley Park is probably my favorite walk, that or Lost Lagoon," she told him.

"Cretkit jubjub bird and the frumious snootchem."

"That's nice too."

When a nurse came into the waiting room and asked who we were here to see, the bald man stood up and said very clearly: "They're here for Randy, he should be out by now."

The nurse couldn't tell us what Randy was coming out of, he didn't know. The bald man led us to the game room then returned to the waiting room, to welcome more visitors I guess.

Randy was standing by a card table, staring into space. He had not come out of wherever he was. His eyelids paused when they blinked. His face was slack, he didn't seem to know who we were. They were giving him shock treatment— electroconvulsive therapy, ECT. I was told by another doctor that ECT wasn't effective for schizophrenia, but my parents had to sign off on all prescribed treatments at Essendale if they wanted Randy institutionalized.

"Hi, Rand," Mom said. She patted his upper arm and then squeezed it, taking note of how thin he was.

"Hi, Mom, I just had to go to see *th uh su uh* . . ." His sentence lost wind as he spoke until his words were inaudible. He sat down at a table and started shuffling cards.

In describing the shock treatments, Randy's doctor had

said, "The mind is like a deck of cards. Sometimes it gets stuck handing out the same top cards. ECT gives the deck a reshuffle."

"What if the new top cards are worse?" I asked him.

He said I was missing the point.

From what I could see, Randy's new cards weren't better. They electrocuted his brain once a month and gave him tranquilizers the rest of the time. Everybody else in the room was old. The air was old. He was nineteen. I asked if we could go outside, even though it was pouring. Better that it was pouring. But Randy said he'd already been out for the day. He dealt us each three cards. Mom picked hers up, ready to go along with whatever the game was. I asked what we were playing, but then Randy snatched the cards back from us and started shuffling again. His eyes became more focused as he watched the cards, dealing us each three, one more time.

"What's that?" he asked, pointing to a small gold crucifix I was wearing. I'd found it in the women's bathroom at a restaurant I was singing at.

"It's just a necklace I found."

"It's a cross. Why are you wearing a cross? What does it mean to you?"

"Nothing, it's just pretty. I like it."

He took the cards back and reshuffled.

"You shouldn't wear a cross if it doesn't mean anything to you."

Randy had gone through his Bible phase before his illness. But it never seemed like he was reading the Bible, just carrying it around like a prop to let us know he was not the same person as before.

A nurse drifted over and gave Randy a look to shush him. Randy shuffled the cards more.

"Three card stud," he said, tossing different cards in front of us.

"Okay" Mom said, with forced cheerfulness.

He grabbed some poker chips off another table where some senile old men were hunched in a circle. They raised a fuss, the nurse shook his finger at Randy, but in seconds the men forgot what they were complaining about and we all anted up. I asked for a card but Randy was playing a game of his own invention. He placed my card in his hand then glared at me. Was he waiting for me to come up with the right move? His skin was beige, malnourished. I looked at his tortured eyes—accusing, resentful, pleading. Brother, not my brother, stranger, my closest friend, crazy person.

Would he come back?

"You lose!" Randy said, raising his voice, then he yanked the necklace off my neck, accidentally grabbing some of my hair, which made me yelp.

Now the nurse was in Randy's face. "Randy," he said, low and threatening.

"It's nothing." I tried to smooth things over. "It was my fault."

Mom's mood crumpled.

"Game's over. You lose," Randy said, and he walked away.

When he reached the door of the hallway, he shook the necklace and yelled again, "You lose!"

My basement room was dark and private, perfect for studying and running lines. When I needed a break I would pull open the curtains to let the sun in. No one ever disturbed me, except to summon me to dinner. But one Sunday, after she'd returned from church, Mrs. Greer knocked on my door.

"Do you have a sister named Marlene?" she asked.

I did.

"She's quite distressed."

I went up stairs and picked up the phone but there was no one there. I wanted to go back and finish the last chapter of *Crime and Punishment* because I was being tested on it the next day, but Mrs. Greer insisted we go look for Marlene. "She said she was hiding by some totem poles. I imagine that would be in Stanley Park."

I don't know how much Mrs. Greer knew about my family, I never spoke about them and she never pried. She was just a person who was always ready to help anyone in need.

We drove to the park and made our way through the herd of tourists gawking at the brightly colored totem poles. I quickly spotted Marlene at the base of a tall pole dominated by a thunderbird with outstretched wings. She was leaning her back against a grizzly bear holding a frog, which gave the illusion that she was being held. When I called out, she ran to me as if the totem animals had come to life and were chasing her. She was on something.

As we drove through Shaughnessy and turned into the Greer's long driveway flanked by twelve-foot hedges, Marlene's eyes started spinning. Through the grand foyer, past the formal dining room, and into the sitting room—she cowered like she was expecting to be ejected any second. She couldn't be sure what she was seeing was real. I was desperate to study but now I couldn't abandon her. We walked around the neighborhood and she kept saying things like, "Wow, you really hit the big time," and "You sure got it made now."

I took her to a Tim Horton's and spent a long caffeinated night talking her down. She'd come into the city with a friend who must have slipped her a hallucinogenic, then somehow they got separated. Fortunately she or someone had written the Greer's telephone number on her hand. By morning she was almost stable. Mrs. Greer drove her to the bus depot and we gave her some money to get home.

Before dropping me off at school, Mrs. Greer told me how she used to take pills to stay awake when she was nursing. "It was very common with nurses and doctors," she said. Her Scottish brogue made everything she told me sound like a wise old tale.

"Well, that turned out to be speed I was taking. I understand a person can take drugs without knowing what they're getting into."

I met John Gray when he cast me as the Red Queen in *Alice in Wonderland* at school. We became close friends after he chose me to play Charlotte Corday in *The Persecution and Assassination Of Jean Paul Marat As Performed By The Inmates Of The Charenton Asylum Under The Direction Of The Marquis de Sade*, better known as *Marat/Sade*, by Peter Weiss. I was playing another crazy. We watched the film directed by Peter Brook and it was tempting to imitate Glenda Jackson, but that was all too Royal Shakespeare for me. I had an organic connection to mental illness. I confided in John about Randy, and he facilitated my exploration without making me feel unsafe. My character was narcoleptic, something I could also relate to because of my long stretches of sleeping through depression. The play was intellectual, with extensive passages of philosophical back-and-forth between Marat and the Marquis de Sade. I swallowed up everything I could read about the French Revolution. I had always been told we were descendants of French aristocracy, and maybe my ancestors became Girondists like Charlotte Corday. I felt it in my DNA. I gave myself lots of air to let the sound of my voice come from deep down. I didn't think of the meaning of the words. I created mental pictures—I gave myself the placid face of my grandmother, with her volatility just under the surface. Being surrounded by lunatics was not a stretch. The play was also a musical, or rather it had song interruptions, and I loved the music.

When I came with a knife concealed in my bodice to kill Marat who was described as short and deformed, with a terrible skin disease, I imagined taking vengeance against the beastly little Greek man.

Home for the Holidays

Dad sometimes quoted Bertrand Russell—"Christmas is an insult to the poor"—to make our uncelebrated holiday seem like an ideological choice. But being with the Greers while they trimmed their tree with homemade decorations—weaving a wreath of cedar branches, bells and sprigs of holly, and stringing up greeting cards—I started to wonder if Christmas could actually be pleasant, a time for family to just be together in an affordable way. I decided to buck family tradition.

I called Mom and she agreed that it might be nice to bring Randy home for Christmas. I had saved some money from passing the hat and I loaded up on cheap gifts from the Army and Navy store. I stuffed everything in my duffel bag and toted it, along with my guitar, through the slush and jingle of the city to the bus, to the ferry, and all the way home.

Dad had chopped down a silver fir from the side of the road by the Robert's Creek cemetery on his way back from the beer parlor. One side of the tree was full, while the side that faced out the window to the post office parking lot was misshapen. Everyone who picked up their mail in Gibson's Landing would see it at some point during the week, but such things didn't matter to me anymore.

Randy was sitting in the big chair, pushed to the furthest corner of the room from the tree, shrouded in cigarette smoke. Dad's artist friend, long tall Fred Carney, was lying on the floor beside Randy. On TV, Mary Tyler Moore was having a charming tiff with her boss, Mr. Grant, but Randy and Fred's eyes were glazed over.

Dad and Mom were having a spat in the kitchen. There was the smell of something burning.

"Hey," I said.

"Hi, I'm Fred," said Fred, stretching out a sinewy arm.

"I know. I modeled for your art class." It was torture, I was thirteen. My face blushed and eyes watered for three hours straight, four nights in a row. Fred apparently gave the sixteen dollars I earned for that to Dad. It never got to me.

"Of course, Barbara. You've gained a little weight. Beautiful though. Beautiful girl. I'm a little out there, haven't slept for four days."

"Oh, sorry."

"No, no. It's an experiment, I want to see what happens to my mind after a week." He grinned a loony grin and his eyeballs looked like they were spinning in their sockets.

"How are you, Rand?" I asked, my good cheer a little pushed.

His mouth went hard and he glowered at me. "Never been better," he said.

Mary Tyler Moore held our attention for a moment with

her loving complaints to her husband. "Oh Rob," she whined. "Oh Rob!" Randy mimicked her. Fred laughed, he had the manner of an oversized capuchin monkey.

There was a shout and clatter from the kitchen then Dad skulked out with his shoulders up by his ears.

"Oh Rob," Randy said, and Fred laughed some more.

"Pork and beans tonight," Dad announced. "Save our appetites for tomorrow. Hi Barb, you're looking a little Rubenesque."

"No, no. Ruben's women were fat and lumpy. Barbara's lush and lovely, like a Vermeer," Fred said.

I made a mental note to stop eating so much dessert and to look up Rubens and Vermeer.

"Gonna play 'Silent Night'?" Dad asked.

"Maybe later."

I laid out the items in my Santa sack. Kate and Bobby came bounding through the door, all wet and flushed from grass hockey in the slush. They squatted under the tree counting presents.

I asked Randy if he could help me put the lights up, but Fred jumped in, thinking he was doing me a favor. Dad had an array of found sea glass pieces that he wired to the branches. They were crude but when the lights shone through them they looked like something the three kings might have carried to Bethlehem. Randy watched. His mouth softened a bit and his eyes looked more focused.

Mom came out as skinny as ever and tired from a long day, still in her waitress uniform.

"Hi, Barbara." She waved. Her nylons had dabs of pink nail polish above the heel to stop the runs from moving up.

Her white shoes had been painted a hundred times, but she couldn't cover up the fraying at the seams.

"Okay kids, dinner's ready."

She sat on the arm of Randy's chair and whispered something to him. He leaned in with his head down and whispered back.

We ate canned pork and beans around the TV. The intended lasagna had not been tended while Mom was at work and had dried up like leather. I didn't mention that I no longer ate meat and just picked around the pork bits.

Marlene stopped in for a minute with a friend. Both had identical eyeliner and embroidered bellbottom jeans, and they giggled non stop. She was staying at her friend's place and would come by in the morning. Fred ate all the blobs of pork fat I left on my plate.

Later I strummed out some carols. When I sang "Silent Night" Fred started snoring. Sleep in heavenly peace took on new meaning and we laughed. Dad passed around eggnog. His and mine had a strong dose of rum but no alcohol for anyone else.

Then he started a round of "The Twelve Days of Christmas." He actually got Randy saying "a partridge in a pear tree" each time. When no one could remember the lines Dad would make them up—eight whores a hoping, seven dogs a humping, six bums a bumming, five golden rings—like he was Mario Lanza, an opera singer he liked to ridicule. Kate and Bobby passed out on the couch, and we all found our spots to sleep. Fred's snoring rattled the house all through the night.

Early in the morning, Kate and Bobby were up shaking

and squeezing packages, calling out for everyone to get up. Fred was still on his back snoring.

Dad was fixing breakfast, shirtless and barefoot in his dungarees. His neck was almost black from working outside. The rest of his torso was pale mocha. He drank a lot of beer but had no excess weight on his body. He cracked eggs for pancakes with one hand and then crushed the eggshells and put them in the coffee pot. That's how he made tugboat coffee, by pouring boiling water over the grounds and settling them with eggshells. Mom was in a sunny mood, relaxing with a cup of creamy coffee. Dad started whistling, "Someone's in the kitchen with Dinah," and flipped flapjacks high in the air.

"Merry Christmas, hohoho."

Everyone converged on the kitchen. Marlene floated in, and Randy came out of his old room looking pretty normal.

Dad handed him a plate stacked with food and said, "My gift to you."

Randy smiled, not sardonically or resentfully. It was a good moment.

Dad presented each of us with a plate, saying, "My gift to you."

All seven of us squeezed round a table built for four, elbows overlapping, dripping maple syrup, the low rays of winter sun bouncing into our eyes. I wish I had a picture, it was the rare time we shared a meal, and the last time. I've probably idealized it in my memory, but I know I felt whole, like when Granddad was with us. Randy and I remembered Bear Creek, the booming grounds, the garbage dump, the beach, the main hall and church. The kids were fascinated by our tales of bears and cougars, and of the creek where I abandoned Marlene, and the helicopter in my eye. We talked about when I threw a dart in Kate's head in Rosedale and I bribed her with candy so she wouldn't tell Mom, and the time Kenny Person put his mitt in front of my face to catch a line drive then dropped it and I got a broken nose. There was not one bad moment until it came time to open presents. I wish we had skipped that part. Randy sat in the far corner. Fred was still asleep but at least he'd stopped snoring. Bobby scurried over with a gift wrapped in handpainted newsprint that he'd made himself. Randy nodded and held it on his lap.

"Open it," Bobby said.

"I don't have anything for you," Randy said. He'd been locked away for three years, he wouldn't even know what to buy if he had money.

"That's okay. Open it!" Bobby insisted, but Randy didn't respond.

Mom called Bobby over to open a box, the prize gift, a set of darts with rubber suctions on the tip so you couldn't "puncture skulls with them." But it wasn't funny anymore. Randy got the biggest pile of presents. I'd bought him a sweater and a shirt, and I had wrapped up my hardcover of *Crime and Punishment*. Bobby laid packages in front of him and waited. Finally he asked if Randy wanted him to open anything for him. Randy shook his head and stopped having eye contact.

Bertrand Russell was right, Christmas was an insult to the poor.

We opened the rest of our gifts quietly, trying to salvage the day for the sake of the kids. I got a James Taylor song-book. The sweaters I'd bought didn't look as nice as I had hoped but maybe it was because no one was smiling. Randy was in the Arctic Circle, his mouth turned down, our words drowned out by polar winds.

The kids went out to run around while Mom started dinner. I was in the basement learning to play "You've Got a Friend."

Several hours later, Mom came down and asked if I'd seen Randy. No one had. Fred was gone too, but then we found him at the bottom of the back stairs breathing in cold air, clueless.

Mom and I drove around the rest of the night looking for Randy. The temperature dropped. The roads iced over. Christmas lights kept vigil over sleeping homes. Randy's pile of unopened presents was still sitting in the same place the next morning. Boxing day. I was missing money from my purse, but not enough to take him very far.

Mom didn't want to call the RCMP. It was Corporal Johnson who'd taken her away in a straightjacket that time she'd flipped out at the ferry terminal. Dad tried to reassure her, saying Randy had probably gone to visit a friend. But he had no friends to visit.

Somebody said they'd seen him on the ferry Christmas night, but didn't see him disembark. The rumor that he'd jumped overboard took root.

I went back to the Greers with my empty sack, eager for winter break to be over so I could immerse myself in school again.

Mom got this notion that Randy had gone to Jasper to look for work as a park ranger, like her dad. I went to the Vancouver Police Department and registered him as a missing person. I only had a picture of him from when he was four-teen, which elicited sympathy, but when I told them he was a twenty-year-old mental patient they were mostly concerned about whether or not he was a danger to the public. I gave them a detailed description, then periodically over the next two years I would check in. Twice I went to the city morgue to view unidentified bodies fitting his description. Talk about a no-win situation, walking into that room, hoping you don't find what you're looking for.

I pick up the funeral programs—a few less dollars for my getaway. Marlene is coming up the stairs to her apartment carrying a small bag of groceries. Inside Mom seems more agitated than depressed.

As soon as Marlene slips into the little kitchen alcove to make tea, conspiratorial looks pass between Dad and Mom. They gaze over at the birdcage where Max cowers in the cor-ner. Mom shakes her head.

"Do you want a pill, Barb?"

Dad has never offered me drugs before but I'm sure he noticed my teenage pilfering.

"What does it do?"

"It calms you down and lifts you up at the same time."

Marlene glides over and holds her hand out, "Ya!" she says, and Dad dispenses a blue tablet. I take one but hold off swal-lowing it. The kettle whistles and Marlene goes to it.

"Max flew away," Mom whispers. "We had to buy a new one and paint that thing on top of its beak because they had no females."

"What?"

"With a brown felt pen. The males have a blue thing here." Mom points to the top of her lip. "We painted it brown so it would look like a girl."

"It's called a cere," Dad slurs. "*Shhh*," Mom urges.

"Max is a girl?" I didn't know.

"You just had to have your smoke," Mom spits out. At least having Dad to blame keeps her blood moving. She'd be comatose if it was her fault.

The whispers stop when Marlene enters with cups and a pot. Bobby puts his head down, uncomfortable being an accessory to the crime. She hands him a cup.

"None for me, thanks."

"Is that a new teapot, Marlene?" Mom asks.

"No."

"Got any milk?" I ask, to get her out of the room again. I'm curious to view the budgie's cere.

"I just got half and half."

Mom stands between Marlene and the birdcage. "I'll help," she says.

"With what?"

"Do you have honey?" I say.

"Just sugar." She pronounces it "shigger."

"I'll have shue-gar," says Dad, overpronouncing.

Bobby exhales loudly, releasing tension. He moves to the balcony door, which is half open and slips out. Marlene automatically checks to see if Max is in her cage. Mom moves to obscure Marlene's view, a little too deliberately. Now Marlene senses that something is off. She peers around Mom and moves toward the cage. Mom closes her eyes, praying Marlene will be fooled.

The budgie's head is pulled into his chest. Its cere looks brown to me. Marlene peers in. "What's this?" she asks, with panic in her voice about to erupt. She grips the birdcage—"What is this?"—and lifts it off its hook.

Dad steps forward, "Now, now, Marlene . . ."

She screams and shakes the cage like a crazy person. We all shout, "Stop, stop!"

"What did you do? What did you do?" she screeches. "Where's Max?"

Mom is mortified. She says, "He flew away. We got you a new one."

Marlene shakes the cage so hard the door comes open. The bird escapes and flutters frantically around the room.

"This is a perfectly fine bird, Marlene." Dad tries to take the cage from her. She rips it from his hands, runs out to the balcony and hurls it. Down, down, three stories, where it lands on the hedge of the apartment building next door. The bird flies out to freedom and Marlene slides to the ground against the rail. "Get out," she sobs.

We drive in silence. Dad shouldn't be at the wheel but no one has a better idea. When he spaces out too long at stop signs, Bobby says "Go." We're on our way to some all-you-can-eat place, though food is the last thing anyone wants.

After a long lull, Dad opens his mouth, "Poor thing doesn't have a chance out there. Male bird with makeup on is gonna get jumped by crows."

We all sit with that for a while.

I notice Mom's shoulders are vibrating and I wonder if she's crying, but then a muffled laugh escapes. Dad snorts out a chuckle. "Oh stop, Jack," she says, embarrassed, but she laughs again. And Dad joins her. Mom doesn't laugh much, but when she does it's often inappropriate. It's the kind of laugh I have no resistance to.

"The size of a large grapefruit," the doctor said. Benign, but it would have to be excised from my fallopian tube. School was almost over and I was about to start the tour guide job at the Parliament buildings for summer. I had no time for an operation.

I saw the thing inside me, the buried assault under layers and layers of denial.

I was finishing the year doing set design on a school production of *Philadelphia Here I Come*.

At the same time, Mr. Greer was having a medical procedure that I didn't give much thought to. When I came home one night, his niece met me at the top of the basement stairs. "Uncle Cliff had heart surgery today," she said.

"How did it go?" I had forgotten this was the day he was going in.

"He died on the operating table."

I almost fell down the stairs. I didn't know he was sick, he seemed so vital and strong.

Mrs. Greer was stoic, looking after everyone else, while the crutch of religion carried her. It was awkward being in the middle of a family's grief. I didn't have the poise to be supportive, to say how sorry I was without breaking down.

His funeral service was the afternoon *Philadelphia Here I Come* was premiering. I wanted to see the show but the funeral was more important. I had done my work, I was behind the scenes, I didn't need to be there. But I didn't notify the school. The funeral was a big affair with politicians and city leaders making speeches about Mr. Greer's contribution to the community and the country. I was given the status of a family member, sitting in between Beth and Mrs. Greer. After, I helped Mrs. Greer at the reception.

The next day when I returned to school, Mr. Holland gave me hell. It didn't matter what was going on in my personal life, the show must go on.

I was so bruised by his lack of sympathy, I left school that day and didn't finish the year. I went to stay with Mom, who was living in Victoria now.

Then I showed up for the summer tour guide job at the Parliament buildings, but on my first day the pain from the waistband of my uniform pressing against my tumor made me faint under the rotunda. Someone took me to the emergency room and the next day I had surgery. I woke up and Dad was sitting in a chair at the end of my hospital bed. "Well it looks like you lost a few pounds anyway. Maybe a quarter inch of fat all around. They took out your appendix while they were in there."

I slept.

I woke up to Mom spreading a mashed-up avocado on my face. The woman in the kitty-corner bed said, "What the hell are you doing?" and Mom started to giggle like Lucy Ricardo, and I couldn't stop laughing even though the sutures in my stomach were ripping me.

I slept and slept. When I was discharged, I went back to Mom's place and slept more.

I went to see the surgeon for a post-op checkup. I'd only met him when I was unconscious, and he went on vacation before I came to. He barely looked at me as he read my chart. He talked about an "untreated condition, irreversible damage." Then he said, with no kindness, "You'll probably never have children." He had cropped brown hair parted to the side on a face I would forget. I remember there were some kids in green uniforms playing soccer outside, hollering and getting muddy under the sign: Victoria Royal Jubilee Hospital. The word jubilee stuck in my head. My face was burning but my hands were ice. The doctor wasn't looking at me, sitting behind his neatly organized desk anchored by silver-framed pictures of his children who would all go to college, propped up against his wall of diplomas.

I would have made a pact with the devil right then—to be Lady Macbeth incanting "unsex me here." To turn my power-lessness into something dramatic. Mercutio and I were worm's meat. I had no money, no prospects, just a big hole in my middle. Undreamed of babies turned to rock in my unformed womb. "Don't do any heavy lifting," the doctor said. I almost laughed, but instead I whispered, "Thank you." And I crawled back to Mom's couch, where I slept for the rest of summer.

I was getting some September sun on the beach at Thetis Lake, emerging from my somnambulance. I heard my name. Gorgeous Brent was standing over me with his wavy black hair and thick long eyelashes. He was a year ahead of me at theater school. The sight of him hand-in-hand with his pretty blond girlfriend had always inspired a tinge of envy in me.

He asked if he could sit down. I wasn't keen to chat but he blended right into my mood and I told him everything. Some guys might be put off talking about fallopian tubes but Brent was sympathetic. At some point in our conversation, I was gripped by a deep feeling of love for him. In a short time, I was living with him.

John G. invited me to come play a small part in a production of *Medea* his company was doing. I was one of Pelius' daughters who washes him in blood. Suzie Payne played Medea. She was a stunning actress, very tall and powerful, with a face that stretched from beautiful to strange. The company called themselves Tamahnous, a West Coast Indian word meaning the ladder between earth and sky. Dad got them in a panic when he convinced them it actually meant nostril, but they soon caught on to Dad's sense of humor. Most of the members were UBC theater grads. I was the baby.

Brent built an enchanted little loft for us at the top of an old rambling house we cohabited with a gang of messy potheads. I felt loved, taken care of, understood and respected. He went away for a month, sluicing for gold in the Yukon. He had trained to be an actor but turned practical as soon as he left school. All the time he was gone, I missed him terribly. He wrote me long, Rilke-inspired letters. On the night he came back, I was lying in bed waiting, feeling very much in love. His truck pulled up. He was unloading gear, hanging stuff up outside. I cherished how organized he was, echoes of my Granddad.

The front door opened, I was still in love. Then he spoke to one of the potheads. As soon as I heard his voice, some unexplainable chemical event occurred and all my love evaporated. He came upstairs and into our room. I pretended to be asleep. He lit a candle, I could feel its glow on my cheek. He sat watching me for a long time. I couldn't open my eyes and lie to him, so I lied to him with my eyes closed. In the morning, I ran to the bathroom before he woke up, got dressed, ran down stairs, opened the back door to grab my bicycle and ran smack into a moose carcass hanging upside-down.

I was invited to stay on with Tamahnous and moved into a Kitsilano house with Suzie, my old friend Colleen, and a mime artist who lived in the basement mourning her mother's death.

Acting was everything to me. I was beyond grateful for each day I showed up to collaborate with the artists in our company. Every three months we would mount a play at the Vancouver East Cultural Center. I played multiple roles in the Bacchae, inviting audience members to dance with Dionysus. When we performed in men's prisons that was tricky. We performed in schools, churches, and parks. We gave workshops and took workshops.

We did a musical production loosely based on *The Tempest*. It opened with the actors in the formation of a ship, recreating the shipwreck. We sang a bluesy riff—"My name is Bill Shakespeare and I'm a famous playwright, *ooh ooh ooh*." I was Miranda, the figurehead of our ship.

Mom associated artists with hippies, parasitic insects, and drugs. After a life of instability, she wanted order and predictability. But Dad enjoyed coming to our shows and hanging out, especially with the resident potheads.

My housemates had accumulated a trove of pot seeds that were sitting in a ceramic dish on the kitchen window sill. I had stayed clear of marijuana since my early teens. It made me panicky and disoriented. I shared similar sensitivities with Randy and feared the voices might overpower me if I messed around with drugs. So I can't give a sensible explanation for why I decided to take those pot seeds and germinate them, other than I like to see things grow. I spread them on wet paper towels and sealed them in plastic baggies. Within a week they had sprouted and so I threw some dirt in several egg cartons and planted them. When I saw how quickly they grew I didn't have the heart to snuff them out. I collected discarded clay pots from around our yard and our neighbor's yard, and filled them with dirt from a fallow flower garden. I transplanted the seedlings and put them in my bedroom, which had southern exposure.

Soon the plants were overtaking my room. I had to get rid of them but at this point I couldn't bring myself to destroy them, so I drove down to the Frazer River in Colleen's car, with the intent of transplanting them into the wild. While I was readying a little plot for them, I was discovered by the RCMP. I had forty mature plants and was charged with cultivation.

We were in rehearsals for an original musical called *Salty Tears on a Hangnail Face*. It was about a hippie commune. My days were spent singing, dancing, searching for legal representation, and contacting all the respectable figures in my past for character references. I was mortified to approach Mrs. Greer. She would do anything to help me, but needed reassurance that I was not selling marijuana. I felt like a liar and an idiot saying that I was just growing it, that I didn't even smoke it, but it was true. She contacted her friend, the member of Parliament who had little to go on after my fainting spell as a tour guide, but he wrote some impressive kudos. His letterhead went a long way with the judge.

At the courthouse, I introduced Dad to Mrs. Greer. Dad had thrown together a suit jacket and he'd pressed a shirt. He was clear-eyed and humble, his best handsome self. After an awkward start, he and Mrs. Greer started talking about Tommy Douglas and the origins of the New Democratic Party. They sat together chatting right up until proceedings began. I was proud that he was my dad in that moment, and grateful that he had come to support me.

I had lucked out with a sharp lawyer from legal aid, who had received my hefty stack of references. They were sent directly to him, so I hadn't read anything. In his comments to the judge, the lawyer talked about how I'd overcome a difficult childhood with little parental support, and that my promising future would be cut short by a criminal record. All the letters made reference to my "difficult childhood." I didn't want people to write those things. Dad left the courthouse before the trial ended. I was granted an absolute discharge, but I went away feeling I'd saved myself by dishonoring my family.

Dad steers his Volkswagen van in big wide bends like he's navigating a tugboat with no tow. I wish we were all in a boat or in the belly of a whale. That was one of my fantasies for our family growing up, that we were all huddled inside a whale. That, and my "Ring Around the Rosy" chant and vision. Mom one time said that everything that went wrong with our family was because Dad drank. To some extent, I believe that. Who knows what could have been done for Randy's illness, but he might have suffered less.

We're stopped at an intersection. There are no cars crossing.

"Go," Bobby says.

"No, stop." Mom tells him, opening the door. "I'm going to walk home."

Return

One day I got a phone call from Pete the Poet. "Hey, I'm sittin' here at the Alcazar with someone who wants to say hello."

I didn't know who he was talking about.

"Hi, Barbara, how are you?" It was Randy. His voice was tired and dark.

Pete thought he was seeing a ghost. He was sure Randy had jumped off the ferry three years ago.

"He's alive, can you believe it?"

In the hour it took Randy to get to my place, I convinced myself that his time away had set him on his path, erased his illness, that he was finally going to fulfill the role of older brother. I opened the door to a haunted stranger. His face was broken and sad, his mouth curved downward. He said he picked fruit in the Okanagan, tarred roads, worked his way to Thunder Bay and did construction there. He said talking to strangers had helped him more than talking to doctors. He said it was rough in Thunder Bay before he met his friend, whose name I can't remember.

In the picture, they are sitting in front of a globe. They tried to trace their journey but none of the places they'd been were on the map.

My relief that Randy had survived was eclipsed by my dread that I would not be able to help him. All I could do was wash his reeking clothes and let him sleep on the living room floor.

Mom sailed over from Victoria, emerging from the depression she'd been in since that Christmas day he disappeared. She took him shopping for new work boots and drove him around to construction sites looking to get him hired. His friend drifted off. I wonder if he ever made it home.

Dad got Randy a job as a deckhand on a tugboat. It was way above his skill level but Dad thought a challenge would be good and Randy was eager. I don't know exactly what happened—Randy didn't release a towline from a barge at the right time, or something, and the tug almost capsized. It was a disaster that could have been fatal.

Randy skulked away knowing he'd failed Dad's expectations again.

Mom wondered if I could get him work at the theater, building sets or as a janitor. I wasn't going to take the risk. I didn't adhere to the notion that finding a job for Randy was going cure his problems. I rented a room in the home of an actress who worked in our company and Randy moved into the garage. Anna was a single mom and a whirling dervish of optimism. She gave Randy the benefit of the doubt, treating him like he was part of the extended family and he responded in a positive way. With the help of a kind friend of hers, he transformed the garage into a living space. For a few weeks they worked side-by-side crafting a sleeping loft with shelves and cabinets underneath. Randy started getting a healthy sweat on his face. He was showing some color and gained a few pounds. Maybe a job he really cared about was all he needed. One night at the dinner table, Anna praised Randy for his carpentry work. He smiled, she beamed, her eyes twinkled and his eyes came to life. He had such a fine face when it wasn't distorted. I wondered if he'd ever made love or kissed anyone. I heard that Jack M. took him to visit a prostitute once, thinking that getting him laid would set him straight. I didn't hear the outcome but it couldn't have been a good experience.

As Randy connected to Anna, explaining the intricacies of making a mortise and tenon joint, I saw him. That feeling of being whole washed over me.

Then a bowl of green beans shattered on the floor. The bowl was in Randy's hands but it was some cruel poltergeist that threw it to the ground. The harsh break startled everyone. Nobody faulted Randy, but he turned on himself. Swooping up the mess with his hands and slopping it on the table, bloody hands and bloody beans, and shards of glass on a white tablecloth.

I asked him to stop, which just made him more agitated.

He cursed at himself, "Fucking asshole. Clean up you stupid fucking . . ."

Anna got right into his face and said, "Stop. There are children here."

Randy retreated to the garage and we didn't see him much after that. Somehow he got a job in construction.

I was playing Lucy in *Dracula*. The universe seemed to be invoking blood.

Anna had dropped her kids with their dad on her way to the theater. I was late. I hated to be in a rush because I was riding a motorcycle and it was raining. I turned out the lights, grabbed my backpack and helmet, and just as I was closing the front door, I heard, "It's not too bad." Randy was sitting in the dark living room, cigarette smoke hovering like a ghost above his head.

I had to lock up and didn't want him alone in the house.

"Can you just take a look at this?" His head didn't turn, his body swiveled.

"Jesus, Randy, I'm gonna be late. Gotta go."

"It was payday today."

Randy was being paid under the table, I guess someone saw all the cash he was holding and rolled him. He had a stab wound in his stomach. The blood seemed black, not a good sign, but I couldn't see well in the dark. It wasn't flowing, just seeping through his fingers. It was serious but he wasn't dying. The rain was coming down heavier now. The show had to go on. I called an ambulance and left him there.

After that night, I started having the dueling dreams. Sometimes he was sitting stone-faced and stiff-backed, with me standing behind him, pleading with him to let go of the knife. Other times we were facing each other, stalking in a circle, testing our trust.

Randy went back to live with Mom for a while and I moved into an apartment with a boyfriend in our company. He was a talented actor and poet, but he was also a pot addict and I lost interest.

I came face-to-face with Ty at a crowded party. He had blue eyes and a strong jaw like Granddad. He was leaving the party because it was too smoky for him, he hated cigarettes. He didn't see that I was concealing a cigarette behind my back, which I crushed between my fingers, letting the embers crumble to the floor as I walked outside with him.

Ty was a writer and former actor who had just come back from a stint in Hollywood. He had a professional, methodical approach to everything he did. He took photographs of me and helped me put a résumé together. He found my little studio apartment. He built me a bed. He washed my car. He convinced me I should start taking my career more seriously. I think I loved Ty but I knew I'd be leaving. And I was always sneaking away to smoke.

Randy came back to Vancouver and I got him into a half-way house. There he became friends with an autistic Asian girl who was obsessed with him. He brought her to see me in a play called *Eunuchs of the Forbidden City*, originated by the Ridiculous Theatre Company in New York, based on the perverse appetites of the last dowager empress of China. I played a concubine. It was controversial within the group and controversial with the public. We were picketed by radical lesbian feminists because they considered the scenes between the empress and her eunuch an insult to lesbian sex. It was a farce. On the night Randy and his friend came, someone threw a stink bomb in the theater, shouting, "This play insults women!" and people were evacuated. Most of the audience did not come back after the smoke cleared. Randy and the girl sat through it all with blank faces, like it was nothing out of the ordinary.

That girl eventually got sent to lockdown for stabbing a counselor at the halfway house with a kitchen knife, and Randy wandered away. He drifted back and forth between the island and the mainland. He would show up at the theater and we'd all be on alert in case he got disruptive. He never did anything terrible, he would just get up and walk around in the middle of scenes sometimes, or he'd laugh inappropriately.

I was invited to do the play in Toronto. It was time to leave.

Misty is outside the restaurant carrying a tow-headed toddler. I forgot she had kids. Her seven-year-old daughter is sulking behind her, unhappy to be here. She's dark like her father. Dad bends his head to her level and imitates her pout.

"That's your grandpa," Misty says. The girl looks at him with angry eyes then lifts her hand in front of her face.

The toddler with blond hair has innocent green eyes that watch Dad in fascination for some reason.

"He takes after his father, huh?" Dad says. His father recently died of stomach cancer. Misty nods then, with an ironic tone, says, "This is your Grandpa Jack."

I suddenly have an entirely different view of Misty. She's a survivor worthy of respect, a single mom with no safety net. All the bad feelings I've ever had toward her disappear. I pray these little children will always be safe.

Inside, Red is asking the person behind the smorgasbord what they do with the leftovers. Since he lived in India, he can't bear to see food go to waste. The Chinese cook assumes he's suspicious that yesterday's food is getting recycled into today's menu, so he proudly tells him that it all gets thrown out at the end of the day.

"Shameful," Red says.

I load my plate with a vegetable stir-fry. Red orders tea, then eats the leftovers on everybody else's plate while the cook glowers at him.

"Remember Stale Beer Stuart?" Dad chuckles. "He'd walk up and finish off everyone's beer."

"That's probably what killed him," Red says. "Do you remember that mudslide up in Ramsay Arm, Barbara? Or were you too young?"

"I remember waiting to hear if Dad was alright."

"We were all out on the booms working, but Stale Beer Stuart was in bed sleeping off a hangover and he got buried. Don't think he even woke up."

"Along with the foreman's wife," Dad chuckles again.

"Now, now, we don't know that for certain," Red says.

"Well, they found her body in the same bunkhouse and the foreman didn't seem too grief-stricken. And remember Rex, poor macho Rex?"

"Oh yes, the boss's son, he couldn't handle it. Went to pieces didn't he?"

"I think he took up selling shoes after that."

The mirth fizzles.

"I used to finish off beer bottles when I was little, until I choked on a cigarette butt," I say. "I'll never drink beer after that."

"Good for you," Dad mumbles.

"Yeah, I think it's a good thing I don't like beer."

"Yep," Dad says.

"I'm glad I'm not a drinker," I go on, feeling a little drunk.

"Yep, everything turned out alright for you, didn't it?

"Why do you say that?"

"Well, you can't complain, can you?"

"Because I'm not dead?" I'm sorry I said that because now I can't stop. "I've got lots to complain about, Dad. My brother is dead. Your son. I know it's hard to keep track of all your children, but I've never lost a brother. So no—things didn't turn out alright."

There's nothing to confront in Dad's eyes, his hard humor is a front for a miasma of sadness. I feel like I've just stabbed him but he's not going to bleed. I leave. In spite of my skimpy sandals and skirt, I start running. Down the sidewalk, through an alley, along the harbor front, across the Parliament grounds. I run through residential streets, zigging and zagging, no idea where I am. My feet slap the pavement flatly. The vegetables rise in my throat and I throw up on the lawn of a Catholic church.

Back at Ryan Street, Mom sits looking at the drawing of Randy. "I bought him a suit," she says. "His first suit."

Her eyes seem more blue because the white part is so red.

"I can't cry," she says, holding her throat. "The tears are stuck here."

She gives me hot milk and I imagine my bones growing stronger.

"Do you remember in Brandon," she starts, "when he got picked up?"

She shares Randy's last confession, a confession that belongs to someone else, but he had taken on the sins of his tormentors.

The milk sours in my stomach. Suddenly I always knew what had happened.

He was raped by a guard at the detention center. The family blueprint.

"He asked me to help him," Mom goes on. "There was all this blood coming out of his stomach, and he said, 'Help me,' and I couldn't. I was standing in the doorway and I couldn't move. I couldn't even . . . Bobby called 9-1-1 and he brought a towel and pressed it into the . . . into his, until the . . . but he was. That's what he said. He said help me."

In his room, disinfectant hangs over the long nights of smoking with closed windows. I wonder if a paramedic emptied the ashtray while scooping up the waste. Weeks of flop sweat steeped in unchanged clothes as he lay here plotting his revenge, the crud of lost innocence caked around his mouth. The folding closet door has a loose hinge. Maybe it was the force of impact from the rifle's charge.

There are white patches on the wall, like cumulus clouds, where blood has been wiped away. All gone. Sing "Ring Around the Rosy." Ring around your rosy buggered babies.

In the morning, I call the theater. They've been trying to reach me. The woman on the phone lays into me how unprofessional I am, how I'll never work for this director again. When I tell her that my brother has died, she softens, but still asserts I should have called. I can't explain why I didn't. They're very sorry about my brother, but they have decided to recast the role.

I call the airlines and try to get a credit for the flight I missed. "You can't cancel a flight after it's flown," a woman says, incredulous over my stupidity. I tell her my story and she gets sympathetic. "Listen, dear, maybe we can work something out if you want to go standby. No guarantee."

Mom brings the new suitcase she bought for Randy to the front door.

On the sidewalk, my possessions have disappeared. I don't know if it was the garbage collector or a passerby. Maybe the Scotts next door have made use of them.

A long black limousine pulls up looking like a beached whale. We figure it must have taken a wrong turn, but then

Uncle Bill greets the driver. My empty suitcase is slipped in the trunk and we all cram in with kids sitting on laps. Dad shows restraint when he discovers the mini-bar stocked with those little bottles of liquor. I sit back and immediately feel carsick. Bill makes me promise to call him in Toronto. I don't mention I no longer have a reason to go there, just the hope in leaving.

The funeral chapel is small. I appreciate that Dad's friends have occupied the pews, absorbing the emptiness. The reverend says a few words about Randy's short life, that he was a great runner and chess player, how his family loved him. He names each of us, and then, because no one has volunteered to speak, he gives people a moment to read the Shakespeare sonnet I chose in silence. The scanty program is useful. I think the picture honors him.

The reverend reads Psalms 23. "Yea, though I walk through the valley of the shadow of death." I don't mind it. I don't think Randy would mind it.

Dad's head is dropped into his chest. I know he's sober so he must be crying. I've never seen that before. Red puts a hand on his back.

I ask for the coffin to be opened, even though I'm scared of what's inside. Randy would dare me, and I can never pass up his dare.

I am shocked by the perfection of his face. It's an idealized projection from someone who didn't know him. They've rearranged his expression, undone all his living. Somehow, this final death is softer than the rigor mortis of his last few years—all stiff-backed and soul dying, doomed eyes, mouth curdled with disappointment. A stranger has set his eyes to forget what they saw and has pulled the worms from his mouth. He looks so dignified in the suit Mom bought, fit for the man he never became.

A cab is waiting for me outside the funeral home. Dad is encircled by his friends. A collective waft of smoke rises above them. Bobby and Kate flank Mom on either side, her eyes are sealing off the present. Marlene has disappeared with Misty.

I wave goodbye in the general direction where people stand. Red gives me a thumbs up.

The drive is long, the road straight and even. Randy's smooth face has not left my thoughts. On the ferry's top deck the wind blows through me. Parents restrain their toddlers from climbing into the life rafts. Teenagers hold hands with awkward anticipation. An elderly couple clutch the hand rail as they struggle up the metal stairs.

I am holding my empty suitcase, heading into the unknown. At the airport, I stand by and hope.